WALKER SUN BOOKS

Russian Literature

/ A SUN BOOK

Russian Literature

MARCELLE EHRHARD

Professor of the Faculty of Letters, University of Lyons

Translated from the French by Philip Minto

/ A SUN BOOK

Walker and Company, NEW YORK

First published in France as La Littérature Russe,
a volume in the Que sais-je? series.
© Presses Universitaires de France, 1948.

Copyright © this translation 1963 by Walker and Company,
a division of Publications Development Corporation.

Published simultaneously in Canada by
George J. McLeod, Limited, Toronto.

Library of Congress Catalog Card Number: 63–17552

Manufactured in the United States of America

Contents

Russian Literature

Introduction

Russian literature, for long almost unknown in the West, has come in the last few generations to hold unflagging interest for us. In the works of the great Russian writers we discover feelings quite new, and almost strange, for in spite of their debts to the West these works are profoundly original. Because of her geographical position and a number of historical factors, Russia developed largely on the periphery of Europe. The form of Christianity inherited from Byzantium just before the Schism cut her off from Rome, and the Tartar invasion completed her isolation. By the time of the liberation she was already used to being a closed world. Jealous of her position as the "Third Rome" and the defender of the true faith, she felt a mistrust for other European nations that has never been dispelled.

The relations with the West established from the time of Peter the Great affected only a superficial stratum of Russian society. As in the Middle Ages, when culture was the province of a few monks, so in the eighteenth and nineteenth centuries a deep rift separated the aristocracy and "westernized" intelligentsia from the illiterate masses, who remained wholly "Russian." Literature might well have lost its native originality, if this intelligentsia had not been painfully aware of the rift and felt a need to come close to the people, both to instruct them and to learn from them. This contact brought into Russian literature a tone of high seriousness, a rejection of art for art's sake, and didactic tendencies. The realistic study of men and things Russian also stems from this nearness to the people. If the great writers all, in some measure, learned their art from foreign sources, they used it only to portray Russia; the interest they displayed in examining and exploring the human soul led them beyond their own intentions, to a point where they were, in fact, psychologists in the broadest sense.

Through this conscious effort on the part of the intellectuals the gap that kept them from the people was gradually bridged. Since the Revolution such factors as universal education, the unity of all classes in a common task, and the common struggle against the German invaders have greatly furthered this sense of identity, which for long was an illusion. At the same time the national character of Russian literature has been greatly reinforced.

1 / The Oral Tradition

Until recent times the Russian people were almost completely illiterate. Yet although they lacked knowledge of written literature, they were highly gifted with sensibility, imagination and musical sense, and always enjoyed an abundant popular literature handed down by oral tradition—a literature hardly matched anywhere else.

Epic Poetry

Whereas in most parts of the world epic poetry has long been defunct, in the northern regions of Olonets and Archangel there are bards who can still recite the old epics.

Literary criticism has tended to refer to these songs as *byliny* (meaning "true tales"), although they are known to the people as *stariny* ("tales of olden times").

These epics raise many questions. Nowadays it is generally agreed that they are not spontaneous popular inventions, but the work of poets such as the minstrels and troubadours of Western Europe. Known as *skomorokhi,* these troubadours would come from Byzantium and the Slav countries to the south to sing at the courts of princes. They were persecuted by the Church, hostile as it was to all profane entertainment. But during the Tartar occupation and for centuries afterward, they were much in demand at the popular festivals, and their art was passed on to simple peasants. During this time, many songs that had sprung up in the Ukraine were exiled to the extreme north, but continued to tell of their native steppes.

Some bards, such as old Ryabinin, who was brought to St. Petersburg late in the nineteenth century, knew as many as fifty thousand verses by heart. It must be added that this task was lightened by the use of "movable sections" that described the hero saddling his horse, or in battle, or feasting, and could be fitted into many different *byliny.* The verses themselves consisted of three stresses, divided by a varying number of unaccented syllables and ending on two of these. The songs are recitatives on a monotone, without instrumental accompaniment. The first collection of *byliny,* said to be made by Kircha Danilov, appeared in 1804; more comprehensive are the collections by Rybnikov (1868) and Hilferding (1872).

From time to time it has been fashionable to attribute mythical, historical, Indian or Persian origins to the *byliny.*

Recently, more serious studies have detected very varied influences—from Byzantium, the Southern Slav countries and Western Europe, as well as echoes of the Old Testament and the Apocrypha. The *byliny* are grouped in several cycles, of which the most important is one from Kiev. In this, two types of *bogatyr* (a sort of knight-errant) can be distinguished. There are the "older" warriors—who may nevertheless have been more recently invented than the others—such as the giant Svyatogor, who was so heavy that the earth could hardly bear his weight, and who perished through pride in his own strength; Volga Svyatoslavovich, who could change into any kind of animal; and the lusty peasant Mikula, who with one hand could lift a plow that thirty ordinary men could not move from the ground.

The other *bogatyrs* were in the service of Prince Vladimir the Fair Sun—a prince who neither exactly resembles the first Vladimir, the "baptizer" of Russia, nor Vladimir Monomakh. He reigned in Kiev, and was the owner of many palaces and churches, but was continually threatened by infidel armies; being unable to defend himself, he often sought the aid of the *bogatyrs*, frequently only repaying them with ingratitude. The most popular of these *bogatyrs* was Ilya of Murom, a peasant's son who was paralyzed until the age of thirty-three, when he was cured by pilgrims and was thereupon gifted with prodigious strength. Ilya routed the enemy, liberated towns and captured the "nightingale brigand." As a hero he was both bold and sagacious, with no vanity or egoism, and devoted to the defense of Russian soil and the Christian faith. Beside him in the struggle against the infidel were Dobrynia Nikitich, a dragon-slayer who also freed a captive princess, and Alyosha, the boasting, crafty son of a peasant, who was devoted to women and money, but also capable of foolhardy courage.

In Novgorod, a town full of merchants and sailors, the *byliny* differed from those of Kiev. They recount the exploits of Sadko, the rich merchant, who twice visited the King of the Sea, enchanted him with music, and received his treasures in return. They also tell of an adventurer named Vasily Buslayevich.

At a later date, songs appeared in Moscow devoted to Ivan the Terrible in his role of protector of the people against the boyars,* and as the liberator of Kazan. There were even *byliny* about the pretender Dmitri and Peter the Great, though these were decadent forms.

Besides these poems of profane inspiration, however, the Russian people had a wealth of religious songs (called the *dukhovnye stikhi*), written by monks and based on sources from the Old and New Testaments, the Apocrypha and Byzantine legends. In the *Book of Doves* King David explains the creation of the world to Prince Vladimir. Other songs tell of the unfortunate Lazarus and of the rich sinner, of the adventures of St. George and the humility of St. Alexis. They were mostly sung in chorus by mendicant pilgrims, and were always protected by the Church. Their emphasis is on pity for the meek and sinful who are so dear to Jesus Christ.

Tales and Proverbs

Still in the epic manner, but in the more familiar language of prose, are the tales. A number of collections of

* The boyars were great feudal landowners.—Tr.

them have been published since the eighteenth century, notably by Afanasiev. In these, too, connections with the folklore of other parts of Europe and Asia can be traced, and many of their sources are surprising. The popular Russian hero Bova, the son of a king, is none other than an adapted Bueve d'Antone. But if a number of Western themes are present, all are treated with a typically Russian blend of realism, poetry and humor. The humiliated monk, the simpleton, the orphan girl are always the ones who attain happiness. The sorceress Baba-Yaga may fly through the skies in a pail, but prefers to remain in her forest hut, which is mounted on chicken bones and pivots around so that visitors may enter. The dragon, rather than devour the princess, prefers to marry her and have children. The queen gives birth to a child after eating a pike with golden fins, and the princess hides under the feathers of a swan. The animal kingdom, whether of legendary or of real beasts, such as the wolf, the bear or the faithful horse, is one with the human world. The usual backdrop is the forest or log cabin, inhabited by goblins.

The Russians also have a treasure house of sayings and proverbs. Some of these arise from historical events ("An uninvited guest is worse than a Tartar"), from aspects of peasant experience ("Spring is beautiful, but hungry"), from common sense, or from religious thinking. Numerous sayings combine magic and religion in order to heal diseases of men and animals, or to protect harvests, homes and travelers.

Lyric Poetry

Famous Russian choirs have familiarized the people of the West with the incomparable charm of Russian songs. Some of these date from legendary times; others come from the written literature but have been adapted by the people. The former are invariably without rhyme, their stresses divided by an irregular number of syllables.

The Russians have songs for every occasion, and these form the accompaniment of their dances. There is a song for every feast day; there are songs for spring, and Christmas carols that are sung from door to door, or to enliven the traditional rites of telling fortunes. Sometimes the words have little meaning, but suggest the flight of a bird, a horse racing over the steppe, the whiteness of the birch, fiery-red berries of the rowan tree, or the swirl of the snowflakes. Love songs are nearly always sorrowful, especially those of the young girl about to be taken by marriage away from the home of her fathers; she and her friends implore her father not to hand her over to strangers, and call on her brother to protect her. Country weddings follow ancient rites, sometimes imitating a primitive abduction, and may preserve some of the marriage customs of boyars during the Middle Ages. These rites, accompanied by songs, are tantamount to dramatic shows, but almost magical importance is attached to them. Also sad are the songs of soldiers, which in old Russia would be final farewells to their village and loved one. Then there are laments for the dead, unchanged over the centuries, and threnodies sung by mothers and wives who have lost their "falcon," their "light," and who are now condemned to misery.

The musical wealth of these songs, with their joyous or sorrowful rhythms, and the beauty of Russian voices, which blend so well in chorus, show this incomparable lyrical heritage at its best.

The Popular Theatre

The *skomorokhi* certainly put on farces and perhaps even short dramas, but we have no information about these pieces, which the Church rigorously repressed. Later on, religious dramas, which had been given in Church academies during the seventeenth and eighteenth centuries, were adapted for the popular taste.

The puppet theatre, imported from Germany, had the mischievous Petruchka as its main character, and had a place in every kind of fair.

2 / *Literature Before*
Peter the Great

Before the Tartar Invasion

The Christian religion was the cradle of civilization in Russia, as it was in the West. For centuries the flickering lamp of culture was kept alight only by monks.

The fact that Russia derived her faith from Byzantium had incalculable consequences. She might well have inherited the Greek tradition, but ecclesiastical mistrust reduced this to the teachings of the Church Fathers alone. She was deprived of all contact with the classical Latin world, and with the ideas of the Middle Ages and the Renaissance. The tongue used by her first apostles, the Bulgarian dialect known as Church Slavonic, into which

Cyril and Methodius translated the Scriptures, had the enormous advantage of being understood by most Russian peoples; on the other hand, scholars were denied the knowledge of antiquity that the use of Greek or Latin might have given them. The Mongol invasion isolated Russia completely, and for centuries she was to live on the store of literature that had come to her from Byzantium before 1240, mainly conveyed through the Bulgarian Empire, which had reached its zenith in the tenth century. There was an abundant literature of edification, consisting of Gospels and Apocrypha, sermons by St. John Chrysostom and St. Basil, and Lives of the Saints. To this may be added Byzantine chronicles, echos of the Trojan Wars, of Alexander the Great, and of the Roman emperors. All this was copied out in the monasteries, in a language that was gradually deformed until it resembled spoken Russian, and then, hybrid though it was, remained the literary language of the country until the eighteenth century.

The oldest Russian manuscript, richly illuminated, is the *Gospel of Ostromir,* named after the dignitary for whom the deacon Gregory copied out, in 1056, extracts from the Gospels, to be used on Sundays and feast days. The *izborniki,* or miscellanies, prepared some years later for Prince Svyatoslav, contain pages from the Church Fathers, Lives of the Saints, a history of the Roman emperors, and even a treatise on rhetoric.

Already the Russian capacity for emulation was in evidence. Preachers prepared sermons in the style of St. John Chrysostom, and what is of far greater interest, chroniclers recorded the history of the country in the Byzantine manner. About 1115 the so-called Primitive Chronicle (ascribed to the monk Nestor) was written in a Kiev monastery, and this was often recopied and enlarged upon. The earliest extant manuscript of it, the work of the monk Laurence of Suzdal, dates from 1377. Going back as far as the Flood, the chronicler traces the descent of the Slavs from Japheth and retails the legend according to which the apostle Andrew visited Russia. But the narrative becomes really interesting when it describes events close to the chronicler—the foundation of Kiev by the Varangians, Olga's revenge over the Drevlians, the death of Oleg and the conversion of Vladimir, who baptized his people in the Dnieper after having toppled the statue of the god Perun. These half-real, half-legendary happenings are told with animation, color, clarity and an obvious pride in Russia and in Christianity.

Fascinating on account of the details it gives about the life and habits of the time, as well as the insight it offers into the remarkable personality of its author, is the *Testament* by Vladimir Monomakh (1054–1125). Addressed to his sons, it contains religious and moral precepts and wise counsel on the duties of a prince, and is embellished with personal memories. The author emphasizes the hospitality that is owed to strangers and the advantages of education.

At this time there were still contacts between Russia and foreign countries. Monks often undertook long pilgrimages, of which the more literate of them left accounts. Sometime between 1106 and 1108 * the abbot Daniel went to Jerusalem and was well received by King Baldwin. He described the holy places, especially the Church of the Holy Sepulchre, with great accuracy; he attended the Easter eve service and witnessed the miraculous fire from

* Mvishy gives 1106–1108.—Tr.

heaven that lit the lamps of the Orthodox, from whom the Latin Church had to beg fire. Daniel was a proud son, not only of the Eastern Church, but also of Russia, for at every shrine he prayed for his country and its princes.

Another description, of the religious buildings at Byzantium, by the archbishop Antony of Novgorod, is the more precious because his journey there, in 1200, took place not long before the sack of the city by the Crusaders.

The very famous *Lay of Igor's Raid* is an account of an ill-fated expedition undertaken in envy of his renown by two cousins of Prince Svyatoslav—Igor and Vsevolod—against the Polovtsians: after a bloody defeat the two princes were taken prisoner, and the infidels invaded and ravaged Russian soil, though finally Igor did manage to escape. In this work there are many elements. Written in a poetic prose sometimes very lovely but sometimes obscure, it contains descriptions of battles and scenery, Slavic myths and Christian ideas, mature and patriotic political sentiments and one splendid lyrical passage, the lament of Igor's wife, who stands on the ramparts of Putivl and accuses traitors of having caused the Russian downfall.

The authenticity of the *Lay of Igor's Raid* has been questioned. The only known manuscript of it, which was published in 1800 by Count Musin-Pushkin, was burned in the fire of Moscow, so that no examination of the text is possible. The work may be a hoax like MacPherson's Ossian (to which it bears some resemblance). Its main source of inspiration was probably a fifteenth-century poem, the *Zadonchtchina*, an account of the battle of Kulikovo normally considered by Russian critics a copy of the *Lay of Igor's Raid*. It is possibly the other way round.

The Tartar invasion proved a cataclysm that tragically interrupted the evolution of Russia. There followed two centuries of servitude that, although the conquerors imposed neither their administration, language nor religion, completely demoralized the country. From the intellectual viewpoint, this was not only a period of stagnation, but of actual regression. By the fifteenth century, almost all the boyars were illiterate, and many priests, not knowing how to read, had to learn their offices by heart.

After the Liberation

When Ivan III finally asserted his independence by refusing to pay tribute to the Tartars, who were by now too feeble to exact it, Russia was entirely transformed. Independent principalities no longer existed. The great princes of Moscow brought the Russian lands together under their authority, and since Constantinople had been reduced to slavery, Moscow, now free, intended to take its place as the capital of true Christianity. In this it was helped by refugees from Byzantium and from the Slav states to the south. A new wave of culture arrived from the same source as the previous one, and there were even slight ripples from the West. The architects of the Kremlin were Italians, and a disciple of Savonarola known as Maxim the Greek (though he was, in fact, of Albanian descent) was summoned by Vassily III to scrutinize the Russian translations of the Scriptures. This was a perilous assignment, which provoked the protests of the clergy and eventually led to Maxim being banished to a remote monastery. But he had had time to sow the seeds of new ideas. Even the *Stoglav,* an account in one hundred chapters of the decisions of the Provincial Council called by Ivan IV in 1551—a Council full of the enemies of all reform—acknowledged the need for an educated clergy. To prevent further corruption of the Scriptures by fumbling copyists, the first printing press, for the use of the Church alone, was founded in Moscow in 1553. Many chapters of the *Stoglav* throw curious light on the ignorance, barbarism and superstition of the period.

More interesting for the study of the period is the *Domostroy,* attributed to the priest Sylvester, a counselor of the young Ivan IV. (*A Father's Instructions to His Son,* added to the text, is the only work definitely written by Sylvester.) The *Domostroy* is a handbook for the model head of the house. It teaches him how to go about his religious duties, how to behave toward his wife, children and servants, and how to manage his financial affairs without sparing his hospitality. It also contains instructions on making clothes and beer, as well as laying in food for the winter. A rich household was at this time a separate economic unit, living on the produce of its land and the labor of its serfs. The head of the family was responsible only to God, and his authority was reinforced by the whip: according to the *Domostroy,* he could and should use this on his wife, on condition that he did so in private; it was his duty to flog his children and servants because, by mortifying their bodies, he might save their souls.

In this same period there appeared another work, which for centuries was to play a considerable part in Russian religious life. This was the *Chetyi-Minei,* a vast compilation prepared by the metropolitan Macarius, of the lives of prophets, apostles and saints both Greek and Russian, accompanied where practicable by their works, all placed in the order of their feast days. This Summa of all Russian religious writing also contains other works of piety and even tales of pilgrimage.

But the most remarkable writer of the time of Ivan the Terrible was undoubtedly the Tsar himself. His intense and complex personality is shown forcefully in a letter to the abbot of the St. Cyril monastery, and two letters to Prince Kurbski, who, after distinguishing himself in the Tsar's service, had fled to Poland, and in violent missives denounced Ivan's crimes. For his part, the Tsar heaps ironies and insults on the renegade, and quotes any number of biblical passages to support the divine origin of his sovereignty and his rights over the life and death of his subjects. At the same time, impelled by the strange necessity of vindicating himself in his own eyes, he goes over his past, dwelling on the privations and affronts he suffered at the hands of the boyars during his youth and the treachery he had to repress. This is a psychological document of the first importance.

Prince Kurbski himself, in his letters and a *History of the Prince of Moscow* (refusing him the title of Tsar), also traces the development of Ivan's character, from the brilliant beginnings of his reign to the bloodbaths of his later years. Kurbski shows himself a cultured man and a disciple of Maxim the Greek. Able to appreciate the culture of the country of his adoption, he still yearns for his native land.

There followed a "Time of Troubles," of civil and foreign wars and of misery, during which Russia progressed little. Nearly a century after Kurbski, another exile named

Kotochikhin, who once worked in the Chancellory of Foreign Affairs, lived in Sweden, where he wrote a study *On Russia During the Reign of Alexis Mikhaylovich*. This paints a somber picture of the court of Moscow, with its swaggering and ignorant boyars and its savage customs. Another writer, the Croat Kryzhanich, came to Russia with the dream of uniting the Churches and of unifying the Slav peoples. Sent off to Siberia to reflect on his wasted illusions, Kryzhanich also complains, sometimes in Latin, sometimes in a strange mixture of Croat and Russian, of the ignorance and vulgarity of the Muscovites. In his opinion, only the absolute power of the Tsar could put things right.

The second of the Romanovs, Alexis Mikhaylovich, actually did attempt to lift his people out of their barbarian conditions. In the religious field he took up the work started by Maxim the Greek, and under the stern impetus of the patriarch Nikon the Scriptures were revised. Certain usages, like the pronunciation of the name of Jesus, the sign of the cross, and the number of hallelujahs sung, were altered so as to revert to their original forms. But to the people, suspicious of change and foreign influence, this was the work of the devil. The unity of the Russian Church was broken by the *raskol* (schism) and many of the most deeply Christian people were doomed to face persecutions, massacres, flight into the forests, and sometimes even to resort to collective suicide. At the head of the first *raskolniki* was the archbishop Avvakum, who was burned alive in 1682. In his autobiography he expresses his intense faith and his indignation at Nikon's reforms, and tells of his terrible journey with wife and children across Siberia, of the exile and the tortures that his unflinching devotion to tradition had brought upon him. Avvakum's *Life Written by Himself,* which makes use of the vernacular with passionate eloquence, is the most moving work in ancient Russian literature.

But the past, however venerable, had to give ground under the pressure of the new age. The barrier of suspicion that cut Russia off from Western Europe began to be pierced. It was to Kiev—which, in order to defend Orthodoxy against Polish Catholicism, had adopted the intellectual weapons of its opponents—that Moscow turned for its masters. Monks from Kiev who knew Greek were summoned by Nikon for his revision of the Scriptures. The Moscow Academy, founded in 1682, and soon known as the Slavo-Greco-Latin Academy, was an imitation of the theological Academy at Kiev that had been founded by Peter Mohila some time earlier. In spite of their mistrust of Poland and the Catholic religion, these Academies attempted to vie with the Polish Jesuits, and like them gave literature a place of honor. Simeon of Polotsk, who taught in Moscow, and was tutor to the Tsar's children, not only wrote theological works, but a number of religious and didactic poems in the Polish style, which was quite different from the ordinary Russian verse based on accents. As the Academies, always following the Jesuit lead, arranged theatrical performances on religious subjects, Simeon wrote dramas about the Prodigal Son, and the three young men thrown by Nebuchadnezzar into the fiery furnace. The Tsar attended one of these, but was soon attracted by other shows.

Meanwhile Western culture arrived in other ways. Foreign merchants, mostly Germans, became more and more numerous in Moscow, where, since the time of Ivan the

Terrible, they had lived in a special suburb called the *Nemetskaya Sloboda.* Here they arranged entertainments, concerts and plays similar to those given in their own countries. In 1672, on the occasion of the birth of his son Peter, the tsar Alexis ordered the Lutheran pastor Dr. J. G. Gregory to put on a play based on the Book of Esther for the court, and to construct a new building for the purpose. Thus the first Russian theatre was built. Gregory put on other plays on subjects such as Adam and Eve, and Judith.

The popularity of poetry and the theatre was soon matched by the novel. But just as verse and drama appeared in Moscow two centuries after they developed in the West, so tales of chivalry and adventure were read there long after they had fallen out of fashion elsewhere. These were passed around in manuscript form, since there was no secular printing house before the time of Peter the Great; they were adaptations of varying merit of originals destined for a different society, yet they enjoyed great success. The most amusing of early Russian novels is the story of *Frol Skobeyev,* a lowly and unscrupulous adventurer who succeeds in marrying a nobleman's daughter, thus winning love, fortune and general respect.

3 / The Eighteenth Century

Little by little Russia was becoming Westernized. This process would have been slow but for the revolution brought about by the genius of one tsar. This impelled the country to open its eyes to Europe, and at the same time smashed much tradition, prejudice and suspicion.

The Reign of Peter I

The essential tasks for Peter the Great were to revolutionize the structure of the State, to see it catch up on several centuries of technical arrears, and to make it strong militarily, on the seas, and in trade. Literature mattered little to him, though in several ways he did prepare the ground for it. The alphabet was simplified, printing houses were founded to produce technical manuals, not religious books, and the language was enriched by new words taken from Dutch, German and other sources. The Tsar founded the Academy of Sciences, as well as a public library.

At first, literature was mainly a branch of polemics. One of the Tsar's close collaborators, Theophan Prokopovich (1681–1736), Metropolitan of Novgorod, wrote verse and a religious drama entitled *Saint Vladimir*. But above all, in his sermons and rules of the Holy Synod, he was an energetic defender of the Tsar's reforms, showing a breadth of vision on religious matters that suggests Protestant influences. Against these stood Stefan Yavorsky, Metropolitan of Ryazan, the author of a work called *The Rock of Faith,* who spoke for the traditionalists. Vasily N. Tatischev (1686–1750) was a friend of Prokopovich and a high administrator who traveled abroad, where he became acquainted with notions of philosophy and political economy. The study of these he urged upon his son in his *Testament,* a work in which the spirit of the eighteenth century can be felt. His five-volume *History of Russia,* the first clear, logical and intelligent exposition of its kind, prudently (as the author himself wrote) went only up to the Time of Troubles: completed in 1739, it was not published until long after his death.

From a quite different social level came the curious treatise *On Indigence and Wealth,* which in 1724 was addressed to the Tsar by a rich, self-taught peasant named Ivan Posochkov, a vigorous partisan of education and reform. After the death of Peter, this zeal earned him incarceration in a fortress, where he died. Posochkov was an exception who for long remained unique. Culture was to stay the preserve of the aristocracy, which was unable to absorb the great ideas of Peter the Great. It opposed those reforms that directly threatened it, but rapidly became addicted to the habits and pleasures of the West, which it would no longer give up. Soon it became smart to speak a foreign language. The entourage of Peter the Great spoke German, but at the courts of his successors this was replaced by French.

The Reign of Elizabeth

At this time Russia began its true renaissance, which bore resemblances to the much earlier Western Renaissance. Revolution in manners prompted revolution in literature, which turned its attention from everlasting salvation to earthly life. As a result, its idiom changed, abandoning the old Slavonic and picking up foreign words; it needed to be both purified and enriched; it had to create verse and prose styles. Since they were so urgent, questions of form became prominent. The writers of the time were all primarily concerned with theory. Aware of the part they might play in the scheme of Peter the Great, they gave vent, in a century of imitation, to feelings of national pride and their impatience to rival and soon outdistance the foreigners.

Such feelings are present in the work of Prince Antioch Kantemir (1708–1744), who was Russian only by adoption: he was the son of a Moldavian prince who had been an ill-starred ally of Peter I. His diplomatic career took him while still young to London, and later he became Ambassador in Paris, where he died prematurely. His eager studies of Western science and letters were put to the use of his adopted land. His *Satires,* first published in a French translation in 1749, and in Russian in 1762, paint a colorful picture of Russian life, in spite of the influences of Horace and Theophrastus, Boileau and La Bruyère. He is concerned to correct such Russian faults as ignorance, superstition and the absurd arrogance of the boyars. For all its balanced syllabic meters, his verse is ponderous, and his poetic language is archaic compared with that of his highly interesting diplomatic despatches.

Regular verse, with its alternation of stressed and unstressed syllables, was introduced into Russian poetry by Trediakovsky and Lomonosov. V. L. Trediakovsky (1703–1769) was the son of an Astrakhan priest: he left the Slavo-Greco-Latin Academy and ran away to Paris and Amsterdam, but on his return to Russia was appointed to a post in the Academy of Sciences. Even during his lifetime his prolific literary output was the object of derision, especially his cumbersome translation into hexameters of Fénelon's *Telemaque.* His theoretical writings, which are of a higher order, deal with the principles underlying the French classical school and propound a new theory of versification. In 1735, when he wrote his *New and Rapid Method of Writing Russian Verses,* Trediakovsky championed rhythmical against syllabic verse, though at first he only admitted trochees, the rhythm of popular songs. In 1752 he expanded his theory to allow for iambics; in the interval he had learned from his "rival," Lomonosov, who, though also interested in theory, had real poetic gifts as well. In fact

M. V. Lomonosov (1711–1765) was prodigiously talented, and his universality made him the most representative figure of this Russian "renaissance." The son of a fisherman from the Archangel region, he had grown up in this desolate northern country and had been taught to read by Orthodox refugees of the old school. To pursue his education he left home and managed to enter the Slavo-Greco-Latin Academy; subsequently he was able to study natural philosophy under Christian Wolff in Marburg, and also went to Freyburg, where his capacity both for hard work and for license were noticed. Lomonosov was eventually given a chair in the Academy of Sciences, but at the same time as he was making remarkable discoveries in the fields of physics, chemistry, astronomy and mineralogy he had to wage a continuous struggle against his foreign colleagues. In the first Russian grammar ever produced, which appeared in 1755, and also in a treatise, *On the Use of Sacred Books in the Russian Tongue,* he noted the distinction between the original Slavonic and Russian languages, and put forward an interesting theory about the literary language. In this he detected three styles: the noble or Slavonic style held pride of place, but there were also a middle style, which eschewed all familiar talk but was close to the language of formal conversation, and a low style, which made use of everyday expressions. These three manners could be adapted to various types of literary composition. If Lomonosov's theory was over-rigid, it nevertheless sprang from a genuine feeling for language, and nearly all Russian poets have unconsciously accepted it.

As a poet, Lomonosov tried his hand at nearly every form, but the real worth of this "Russian Pindar" can be seen in his Odes. Putting his poetic, as well as his scientific, talents to the service of his country, he became Elizabeth's official poet. In his religious Odes both his deeply rooted faith and his love of nature are in evidence: a splendid sunrise or the Northern Lights will cause him to reflect on the majesty of God.

Before Lomonosov was dead, however, a reaction set in against his grandiose conception of poetry. Elizabeth hardly resembled the Minerva described by her own poet; the courtiers around her much preferred the more worldly verse of Sumarokov. Alexander P. Sumarokov (1718–1777) was an aristocrat who was educated at the Cadet School, but who devoted his entire life to literature. Even in his Odes and Tragedies, he used the language of the drawing room, and elsewhere launched violent attacks on Lomonosov. In these he was supported by the younger generation. But although Sumarokov wrote much, he excelled in his Anacreontic verses and his fables, rather than the more official Odes. His contemporaries most admired his dramatic works, and their author was bold enough to compare himself to Molière and Racine. During this period the public theatre had come into existence: before it there had only been performances at court, mostly by foreign companies, and in the schools (those given at the Cadet School were particularly lavish). Now a native of Yaroslavl, an actor named Volkov, formed a troupe, and Elizabeth brought this to St. Petersburg, where she built the first public theatre in 1756. Its director was Sumarokov himself, and his works appeared frequently in its repertory. These works employed the methods of the French classical school, and the rude Varangians (in *Khorev*) and the first princes of Muscovy (in *Mstislav*) are transformed into refined heroes after the manner of Racine. Nearly all these dramas took their themes from Russian history, but one *Hamlet* (which had little in common with its original) introduced Shakespeare to the Russian scene. Sumarokov's comedies are imitations of Molière, and use the stock situations and even the traditional names of the French comedy. Often they mock Russian peculiarities, such as the dishonesty of officials, superstitions and Francophilia.

The Reign of Catherine II

Under Catherine II Russia remained under the cultural influence of French classicism. But following the French example, she became interested in the literatures of other lands. From Germany and Switzerland she derived the idyll, and from England the sentimentality of Sterne, Young and "Ossian." At the same time, Russia became acquainted with Western philosophy, and this, which was in conflict with many of the old traditions, caused many Russians to judge their institutions with severity. In this way, public opinion was born.

Catherine herself, although she was later to regret it, played a conspicuous part in this liberation of thought. Rarely, if ever, can a sovereign have held such a position in the intellectual life of her empire. She appears in the guise of a philosopher in her *Instruction* (addressed to a Committee of Deputies who were to draw up a new code), which was largely inspired by Montesquieu, but replaced the liberal monarchy of the author of the *Esprit des Lois*

by an enlightened despotism. Catherine also wrote comedies, comic opera, fables, moral tales and articles, always
moved by the desire to educate her people and convinced
that they could have found no better teacher. It was with
disfavor that she saw the writers, encouraged by the freedom she herself had given them, pursue avenues she considered dangerous.

The first literary reviews had been founded around the
middle of the century by institutions like the University of
Moscow and the Cadet School. The first "private enter-
prise" review, Sumarokov's *Industrious Bee,* appeared in
1759 and was devoted to Russian and translated works.
This example was followed in Moscow by M. M. Kheraskov
(1733–1807), but these ventures had few supporters and
were only ephemeral. The success enjoyed ten years later
by the reviews of Catherine's day is a measure of the cultural progress made. The first of these, *Vsyakaya Vsyat-
shina* ("A Little of Everything") was launched in 1769 by
the Empress herself in the name of one of her secretaries.
Inspired by the example of the *Spectator,* it criticized with
grandmotherly indulgence both the ignorance and superstition of the older generation, and the French mimicries of
the younger. While it attacked unconscientious officials, it
left the institutions of the State severely alone. But the reviews that appeared as a result of this precedent adopted a
quite different tone, especially those of Nikolai I. Novikov
(1744–1818). Although he suffered from gaps in his primary
education, Novikov generously devoted his life to the instruction of his fellow citizens. In *The Drone,* a review that
appeared in 1769, he railed against absurdities and abuses,
against the permanent faults of the administration and the

fundamental flaw in the social structure of the country—serfdom. He had hard words for the despotism of the landlords and described the misery of the serfs. In her own review Catherine protested against the intrusion of journalists into affairs that concerned only the government: Novikov answered back roundly, but could hardly win so unequal a battle, and *The Drone* was forced to cease publication. But three years later Novikov again took up his ideas in *The Painter,* which also had only a brief existence. After that, he published nothing but educational reviews and historical works. He left St. Petersburg in 1779 to settle in Moscow, where with his Freemason friends, notably the university professor J. Schwarz (a follower of Jakob Boehme and Saint-Martin) he established several printing presses to produce the educational books that Russia so lacked. Catherine was highly suspicious of the Freemasons in Moscow, wrongly believing these philanthropic idealists to be in contact with the French revolutionaries. She broke up their group and imprisoned Novikov in the castle of Schlusselburg, from which he was only freed, a broken man, on the accession of Paul I.

Another writer of the time, Alexander N. Radischev (1749–1802), possessed the true revolutionary temperament. Better educated than Novikov, he had studied law and philosophy at Leipzig. In 1790, thanks to the inattention of the censor, he managed to publish his *Voyage From Petersburg to Moscow,* which under its appearance as a sentimental journey after the manner of Sterne, contained uniquely bold attacks on serfdom (the cruelty of which is shown in a series of striking pictures) and against the autocracy, which he threatens with a popular uprising. Catherine read this work with astonishment and alarm. Radischev was condemned to death, but the sentence was commuted to exile to Siberia. Returning from exile after Catherine's death, Radischev committed suicide. His book, of which only very few copies escaped destruction, was only published unexpurgated a century later.

The critical spirit of the eighteenth century was expressed with more constraint in the theatre. It is found in the tragedies of Yakov Knyazhnin (1742–1791), who was influenced by Voltaire. In her comedies, as in her reviews, Catherine II attacked bigotry and the exaggerated imitations of French fashions; some are aimed at Freemasonry and a growing taste for the mysterious. But D. I. Fonvizin (1745–1792) produced the first masterpieces of the Russian theatre. The *Brigadier General* may be only an amusing piece, satirizing the faults of the old and the Franco-mania of the young, but *The Minor* is a vigorous work in which, as in the best of Molière, tragedy lurks under the surface of irresistible comedy. Its plot concerns the upbringing of a provincial youth of good family named Mitrophan Prostakov, but it is dominated by the unforgettable figure of his mother, tyrannical, mean and hypocritical toward her family and her serfs; her love of her son alone saves her from sheer monstrosity. The wise Starodum embodies the author's own common sense.

Extremely popular about this time was the comic opera. The most brilliant piece was *Miller, Wizard, Quack and Matchmaker,* by Ablesimov; it makes ample use of popular customs and songs.

Meanwhile the poets pursued their more lofty tradition. In his dull, classically contrived *Rossiad* Kheraskov tells

how Kazan was taken by Ivan IV, and his *Vladimir* is an
account of the baptism of Russia. But there were also a
number of parodies and mock-heroic poems, such as Vassily
Maykov's *Elysium. Dushenka,* by Ippolit Bogdanovich,
is a graceful rendering of La Fontaine's *Amours de Psyche,*
with some typically Russian ornamentation. And the fable
in the hands of Khemnitser, who was much influenced by
Gellert, embodied morality in a pleasant way.

While Kheraskov, Petrov and others were writing their
triumphal Odes, there was one great poet who was to re-
vitalize the form, Gabriel Derzhavin (1743–1816). Of Tartar
descent—his father was an impoverished officer—Derzhavin
received little or no education and for a long while served
in the ranks of the army: although he became an officer at
the age of twenty-nine, he seemed destined to some obscure
career, when his verses won him the favor of Catherine. He
was named governor of a province, personal secretary to
the Empress, senator and (under Alexander I) Minister of
Justice. But his rigid character and principles meant that
he could not remain long in any of these posts, although
his literary prestige never waned.

As the official poet of Catherine's reign Derzhavin wrote
of its splendors and celebrations, but in a new, more lively,
almost familiar style. Calling her Felitsa (a name taken from
one of her own tales), he praised Catherine, not as a god-
dess, but as a good and intelligent woman whose simplicity,
energy and kindness were in contrast to the arrogance and
laxity of those around her. Catherine was delighted with
this portraiture. But Derzhavin's religious odes, such as
God, or *The Waterfall,* which was inspired by the death of
Potemkin, are descriptive poems in the manner of Pope, with

an elegiac note, however, and a truly Russian wealth of images. His love of nature and of Russian life is best expressed in his Anacreontic poems, in his *Life at Zvanka,* in which the poet tells of a day spent in the country. Derzhavin's work is uneven (Pushkin was to say that it was three-quarters lead and one-quarter gold), and so is his language, which is often careless and sometimes incorrect, although he sometimes has verses of a nobility and grace previously unknown. What he lacks is the sureness of touch that the next generation was to have instinctively, and the deep feelings of the romantics.

The first signs of the romantic movement that was to sweep through the whole of Europe were already apparent. Probably the most characteristic of these was the growing fascination with the country's past history, although little was known about the facts of it, and with the popular songs, although these were adapted to the taste of the time. Between 1770 and 1774, at roughly the same moment as Percy in England, Chulkov published his *Collection of Songs,* preceded by *The Banterer, or Slavic Tales,* and followed by *Russian Tales* (1780–1783), in which the old *bogatyrs* are transformed into the knights of the popular novel library. A Slavic mythology was invented, and there were fantasies about a primitive Slavic poetry with a certain Boyan as its bard. At this moment, providentially, the *Lay of Igor's Raid* came to light! In 1804 the first collection of *byliny* appeared.

The other mainstream of the end of the eighteenth century also came from the West, from Rousseau, Sterne and others, and also corresponded to an instinct in the Russian character: this was the triumph of feeling over reason. The influence of Rousseau was more marked in Russia than in any other country, and lasted until the time of Tolstoy. This was the age of ardent friendships, of platonic love affairs, of reflections on tombstones.

The leader of the younger generation was Karamzin (1766–1826), who had been brought up in the school of Novikov. In 1790, he left on a protracted foreign journey, visiting Germany, Switzerland, France and England; his *Letters of a Russian Traveler* are the result of it. In Germany, which was for him the land of thought and virtue, he met Kant, Wieland and Herder; Goethe, who had returned from Italy, was still for Karamzin the author of *Werther*. In Switzerland he dreamed along the shores of Lake Geneva, carrying a copy of the *Nouvelle Héloise*. Frivolous and revolutionary France interested him more than he dared admit, but he preferred the common sense England of Sterne and Young. In all these countries, he was moved to tears by beauties of nature and acts of virtue alike. This same sentimentalism inhabits his poetry, which is inferior to his prose, and the short novel *Poor Liza* (1792), in which the sincerity of a lower-class girl is contrasted to urban corruption. The sentimental novel had earlier made its appearance in *The Letters of Ernest and Doravra*, by Fedor Emin, and *The Russian Pamela*, by Lvov, but *Poor Liza* consecrated its success and provoked innumerable imitations.

The simplicity attributed to the peasants was also discovered in the past: Karamzin extolled the old Russian virtues in his historical novels, such as *Natalia, the Boyar's Daughter* (1792). These novels formed a transition to his career as a historian, which was to occupy him for the rest of his life. In 1816 the first eight volumes of his *History of the Russian State* appeared, and this he continued up to the accession of the Romanovs, when it was cut short by his death. This History makes brilliant use of the chronicles, and into its scenes men of letters were to dip liberally for the subjects of plays and novels. Its main impulsion is to glorify Russian unity under autocratic tsars, and Karamzin renounces the passions of his youth and attacks Peter the Great for having led Russia away from her true destiny.

Karamzin's language is very different from that of his predecessors: it abandons Slavonic, borrows from foreign languages, invents new words based on Russian roots, and frees the syntax. He was the creator of the modern literary idiom.

He was followed by almost all his own generation: by Dmitriev in his pleasant fables and romances, by Vassily Pushkin in his licentious verse, and by authors of novels and "sentimental journeys." Some objections were recorded, however. These were partly justified by the danger that the language would lose its national character, but the partisans of tradition, led by Admiral Shishkov (who defended the use of Slavonic in a study *On the Old and New Styles*) were in favor of a far more artificial language, which the public would no longer have understood. In the long run the day was won for reform not so much by argument as by the talent of the young romantic poets.

4 / Romanticism

Before Pushkin

At the beginning of the nineteenth century, everyone
in Russia was a poet: in the universities, colleges and military academies the students seem to have spent most of
their time writing verse and founding literary reviews and
societies. Poetry was recited in every drawing room, and
every young lady kept an almanac of poetry at hand. Since
political discussions were forbidden, people made the most
of literary arguments. Numerous reviews appeared: the
Messenger of Europe, founded by Karamzin; the *Son of the
Fatherland,* by Gretch (though in 1812 this was mainly
political, it soon became devoted to literature); the *Polar*

Star, by Ryleev; the *Flowers of the North,* by Delvig; the *Contemporary,* by Pushkin. Though at first they published many translations, original works increased in number. It was only later that greater importance was given to literary criticism: Polevoi's *Moscow Telegraph* and Nadejdin's *Telescope* discussed the principles of romanticism, while the corrupt Bulgarin courted the favor of the authorities by casting a slur on the genius of Pushkin in the *Northern Bee.* Apart from the small group who, together with Kuchelbecker and Odoievski, published *Mnemosyne,* few had any knowledge of German romanticism: the Russians, like their French masters, passionately admired *Werther* and *The Brigands,* Walter Scott and Byron; they saw the passionate and picturesque side of romanticism. Zhukowsky seems to have initiated the trend.

The life and work of Zhukowsky (1783–1852) are infused with pre-romantic sentimentalism. He was the son of a Russian aristocrat and a Turkish slave. Everything combined to arouse in him a melancholy that was to stay with him throughout his life: his insecure childhood, his education at the boarding school for the nobility in Moscow where Masonic mysticism still held sway, the death of a friend, his long and unhappy love for one of his nieces, and her death. The melancholia was not dissipated even by his position as tutor to the future Alexander II, nor by a late marriage that exiled him to Germany. He achieved fame with a hymn written in 1812, celebrating the Russian victories, but he was happier writing intimate and emotional poetry for a few close friends; his gentle, melodious verses tell of friendships severed by death, of the sadness of hopeless love, of awaiting the solace of death, which reunites those separated by life; he lived not in the present but in a past that he idealized, and in a future life to which he aspired. He could not depict reality; his ballads, so much admired by his contemporaries, served only to transpose his own sentiments into surroundings of fantasy. He did some remarkable verse translations, more often than not exactly reproducing the rhythm of the originals, which brought to the Russian people such works as Gray's *Elegy in a Country Churchyard, Lenore, The Prisoner of Chillon,* the ballads of Southey, Scott, Goethe and above all Schiller, the *Maid of Orleans,* the poetry of Hebel and Uhland, La Motte-Fouque's *Ondine,* which he put into verse, and Ruckert's oriental poems. The selection is characteristic: unaware of the Byronic revolt and the philosophy of the German romantics, Zhukowsky continued to express himself through his translations. His old age was peacefully spent in making a complete translation of the *Odyssey* in hexameters (Gneditch had already made a similar translation of the *Iliad* in 1829). The technique of verse writing owes a good deal to him for his widely varied use of meters and strophes and for the melody of his lines, which Pushkin was to inherit.

Although Zhukowsky was in no way the leader of a "school," all Karamzin's pupils gathered around him to answer the attacks of Chichkow and the Society of the Adherents of the Russian Word. The followers of Karamzin—Zhukowsky, Viazemsky, Bludov, Uvarov, Batiuchkov, Alexander and Nicholas Turgenev, Vassily Pushkin and his schoolboy nephew—founded a rival society called Arzamas, whose witty mockery had as its target the conservative advocates of Church Slavonic. In these controversies there was no question of a battle between classicism and romanticism, but rather between the slavophile and the westernized intellect.

The poets of the new school were all schooled in French classicism, and retained something of it even while following the paths of romanticism. This influence is noticeable in Zhukowsky, but even more pronounced in Batiuchkov (1787–1855), who made graceful translations of the Latin poets and, in particular, of Horace. His original work veils classical tableaux with a romantic melancholy, a melancholy that is not a mere literary fashion, but the anguished sincerity of an unfortunate poet who died insane. A similar blending of emotion and classicism is to be found in the tragedies of Ozerov: *Oedipus in Athens, Fingal, Dmitri Donskoi.*

Griboyedov's celebrated play *The Mischief of Being Clever*, sets a romantic hero, who is very reminiscent of the author himself, against a severely classical background. Griboyedov, born in 1795 of an old-established family, belonged to the Muscovite society described in his comedy; he served in the army, then entered the diplomatic service and was sent to the Caucasus and Persia. During a period of leave in 1823 he finished his play, but did not manage to find a printer. Suspected of having connections with the Decembrists, he was arrested but later released and sent to Persia as diplomatic resident. In 1829 he was murdered in Teheran by a mob of fanatics, possibly hired by the English. He was a grave and solitary man, oppressed too soon and too brutally by his contemporaries, and discouraged by the reaction that followed the liberal promises of Alexander; too clear-sighted to share the illusions of the Decembrists, he gave vent to his bitterness in the play that is his only work (apart from a few rough sketches). The main character of the play recalls Molière's *Le Misanthrope,* but this is a younger Alceste: Tchatski, returning from a long journey, is eager to see once more the girl he loves and the country he longs to serve; but Sophia—a vulgar soul who bears no resemblance to Celimene—has fallen in love with a grossly ambitious dolt, and the country is permeated with favoritism, dishonesty, ignorance and futility. The hero spends one day in the house of Sophia's father, Famousov, a narrow-minded and cunning high official, who shows no pity for his subordinate and who bows and scrapes before his superiors and public opinion; this one day suffices to lay bare the high society of Moscow, with its ill-natured gossip, its meanness, its cruelty toward those who disregard its conventions. Like Alceste, Tchatski departs, knowing that he will find happiness nowhere. His bitter and vehement words berate all the vices and stupidities of this high society in which even language is artificial, "a mixture of French and Nijni-Novgorodian." Every cultured Russian is familiar with this free verse, concise but abounding in unexpected metaphor and striking comic effect.

The same vigorous observation and strength of form is found in the work of the great storyteller Krylov (1768–1844), but he is in no way a romantic and his irony is without bitterness. As a child he was poor, and learned more in the streets than at school; as a youth he led a needy and wandering life, working here and there and spending most of his time playing cards. His plays and fables, however, earned him considerable renown, and he spent his last years in comfort as custodian of the Imperial Library. This portly, easygoing bohemian has remained one of the most popular figures of Russian literature. His best plays, *The Fashion Shop* and *A Lesson for Girls*, are directed against the fad of frivolity *à la française*, as were the reviews during the reign of Catherine. His fables are as beloved in Russia as those of Aesop and La Fontaine in Western Europe; in fact, he and La Fontaine have much in common; good sense, good nature, the gift of observation. Like La Fontaine, Krylov placed more importance on the story than on the moral; he also used free verse, less gracefully, perhaps, but with more force and in a more popular idiom. His early fables are adaptations of La Fontaine's. Following these are original works in which all the classes of society appear: the simple or crafty mujik and the deceitful merchant; the unscrupulous official, who is represented either by a fox or, on a higher scale, by an "elephant governor" who allows his wolf-minions to levy a tax of no less than one sheepskin per sheep; the great lord, as proud of his ancestors as the geese are proud of their geese-forefathers who saved the Capitol. Here also is the poet-nightingale, who finds that the foolish prefer the rooster with his strident cry, or who is commanded to sing by the cat that holds him imprisoned in its claws. The fable form, which allowed such freedom of speech to Krylov, could raise his tone and defy (by 1812) Napoleon, satirizing him as the wolf who thought he only had to deal with sheep, but found himself faced with courageous dogs. The fables of Krylov are unequaled masterpieces of their kind because of their concision, the liveliness of the dialogue, their racy popular idioms and proverbs, and the author's occasional creation of new ones.

Pushkin

Pushkin's brilliant genius harmoniously combined all the poetic currents of the early nineteenth century: classicism and romanticism, foreign influences and national tradition, dreams and realism. Everything that preceded him, everything that surrounded him, seems to have been intended to prepare the ground in which the peerless flower of his poetry was to flourish.

His background is full of contrast: his father came of an old Russian family, his mother's grandfather was an Abyssinian on whom Peter I had conferred the rank of general; Pushkin's curly hair and full lips were a contrast to his blue eyes and long straight nose. His parents were well suited to each other and had in common a frivolous attitude toward life. Alexander Sergevich was born in Moscow in 1799, and was brought up by his grandmother and his old nurse, who knew some wonderful stories. But in his mother's salon he first became acquainted with poetry; Karamzin and Dmitriev were frequent visitors, his father and his uncle composed verses and the library shelves were lined with the works of all the more light-hearted eighteenth-century French poets. Pushkin began to imitate them in French, which he had learned as a child. In 1811 he entered the secondary school founded by the emperor Alexander next to his palace at Tsarkoe Selo; there he devoted his attention to literature, and made some firm friends. He used to wander in the parklands of the school and wrote a great deal of verse, the precocious merit of which was highly praised by his uncle, his superiors, Zhukowsky and even Derzhavin. In 1817 he entered the Foreign Office as a civil servant and made the most of the pleasures of the capital; during this period he wrote some light-hearted verses and, in 1820, his first poem, *Ruslan and Ludmila*. This romantic epic echoes in some ways the poetry of the eighteenth century, but is entirely fresh in its fantasy, its liveliness, the charm of its setting, and the vivacious harmony of its verse.

But Pushkin had more serious things to think about; even if he was not a member of any secret societies, he was involved with the Decembrists. His inflammatory epigrams were being circulated. *The Village* and *Ode to Liberty* fell into the hands of the imperial police, and in the spring of 1820 he was banished to Kishinev and then to Odessa, still as a civil servant. The years he spent in the south enriched his talent: he discovered the steppes and the mountains, and on a visit to the Caucasus and the Crimea, the sea and the picturesque charm of strange peoples: in short, the exoticism that the romantics sought in the East. Since at this time he was reading Byron, the exiled Pushkin naturally adopted the disillusioned melancholy of a Byronic hero, which is evident in a series of poems, *The Captive of the Caucasus, The Brigand Brothers* (a fragment) and *Gypsies;* a very romantic poem, *The Fountain of Bakhchisaray*, tells the sad tale of a harem in the Crimea. The evocative references to the South that permeate these poems are also found in his beautiful lyric poems, such as *To the Sea;* others celebrate the poet's love affairs; yet others, such as *The Knife* (in imitation of Chénier), reveal that he had not renounced his political convictions. By his independence of character and his extravagant and irregular conduct he provoked the hostility of the governor of Odessa, Vorontzov, who managed to get rid of him in 1824. Pushkin was sent to one of the family estates at Mikhaylovskoye, near Pskov, where he was to be under police supervision.

He spent two lonely years there with only his faithful old nurse, and his Muse, for company during the long winter evenings. However, he had the comfort of occasional visits from the ladies of a neighboring estate. This seclusion, this closeness to the Russian countryside, made of Pushkin a mature man. From Byron, who could "describe only himself," he now turned to Shakespeare and Walter Scott; to exotic landscapes, he now preferred a pond—"a sandy bank, two maple trees beside an izba"—and the bells of a herd on the white plain; at Mikhaylovskoye Pushkin became the poet of the land of Russia, the national poet.

In his play *Boris Godunov* he revived the past of Russia; it is a historical chronicle after the manner of Shakespeare, in which, breaking with the classical laws, he juxtaposed scenes infinitely varied in setting, manner and style. The dramatic interest is divided between two characters: the tsar Boris, an astute and steadfast politician, whose strength is undermined by the remorse of owing his throne to the murder of a child; and the pretender Dmitri, also worthy of being Tsar, but also haunted by a sin—of imposture. The setting is old Russia: the Kremlin, the boyars, a monastery, battlefields, the public squares thronged with the fickle, excited crowds.

The verse novel *Eugene Onegin* was not finished until 1830; Pushkin began writing it in the South, but it owes a good deal to Mikhaylovskoye. The scene is contemporary

Russia: the young Onegin is skeptical, callous and early disillusioned by life; he arrives gloomy and bored in a Russian village where he rejects the love of an innocent girl, and trifles with the happiness of a friend, whom he kills in a duel. He later falls in love with the girl whose love he had disdained, but she is now married and in turn rejects him. It is evident that when Pushkin started this work, he was still under the influence of Byron, and identified himself with the hero; but later he seems to condemn Onegin's behavior, and his sympathy is with Tatiana, who, though brought up in the French tradition, is nonetheless a young girl Russian to the core and truly of the people, "Russian in soul without knowing why." The first canto recounts a day in the life of a Petersburg dandy; we are then led through the countryside, while the verse describes the Russian character in intimate detail, the traditional courtesies upheld in the seigneurial residences, the popular superstitions shared by Tatiana. This verse novel, as well as being the most melodious poem, is also the first realistic novel in Russian literature.

Thus in his solitude Pushkin discovered the soul of the nation; but he was out of touch with the trend of thought. If he had been in Petersburg he would, no doubt, have taken part in the insurrection of December, 1825; as it was, he was indebted to Nicholas, who had him brought to Moscow, promising to be himself his only censor in the future—a deceptive promise, however, for all his life the poet was to be persecuted by Count Benkendorf, who suspected every word he wrote. Pushkin's yoke became even heavier when, in 1831, he married the ravishing Natalia Goncharova, who obliged him to lead a worldly life, which he found distasteful. Each autumn he would escape to the solitude of his property in Boldino in order to work, and it was there that he wrote his masterpiece.

His work after his Mikhaylovskoye period centered mainly on two themes: Russia of the past and Russian life of the present. He became more and more attracted by history, and was particularly interested in Peter the Great: he collected documents from the archives of Peter's reign, and celebrated his military prowess, his victory over Charles XII and Mazeppa, in the poem *Poltava* (1828). In *The Bronze Knight* (1833) he contrasted the inflexible will of the power-builder with the humble human desire for happiness; and Peter again dominates the theme of the unfinished prose novel in which Pushkin portrayed his ancestor, *The Negro of Peter the Great*. Doubtless because he himself was something of a rebel, he was attracted also toward quite a different character, Pugachev; he did the research for his *History of the Revolt of Pugachev* on the scene itself, along the Volga, and it was to Pugachev that his concise, natural and picturesque *The Captain's Daughter* was dedicated.

At the same time he wrote a series of poems and prose works devoted to contemporary times: short poems, realistic and humorous—*Count Nulin, The Little House of Kolomna,* and short stories. Some of these he collected, in 1830, under the title *Novels of Belkin;* the most important are *The Coffin-maker* and *The Postmaster,* both foretastes of Gogol in their depiction of very ordinary people. In *The Shot* there appears the somber figure of a man bent on revenge, who has some characteristics in common with the brigand Dubrovski (the hero of an uncompleted story), and with the Dostoievskian Hermann in *The Queen of Spades,* a gambler who is haunted by an obsession. The action is fast-moving and concentrated into a few vigorous scenes: the language is precise, simple and elegant.

No other works show Pushkin so close to the Russian soul as his exquisite verse tales; the themes (apart from one) are borrowed from abroad, but the poet has made them totally Russian by telling them in the words and idioms of the people. No other poet has been able to write popular poetry such as this without sounding in some degree artificial.

Pushkin's lyric poetry is infinitely varied in form and inspiration. His limpid language makes full use of all that the Russian language offers: the majesty of Slavonic expressions, the familiarity of the language of the salons, the pungent phrases of the peasant; he made no innovations in meter, but used all the rhythms of his predecessors to create a new music—sometimes grand and solemn, sometimes dancing like a song. His poetry depicts all the aspects of the Russian temperament, from the great to the familiar. It sings of love, whether happy or sad. In his later years, it often expresses a resigned melancholy, a longing for tranquillity, and thoughts of death. Although in his youth Pushkin wrote "liberal" verses, he did not think of poetry as a political weapon; he thought poetry should glide serenely above day-to-day strife and uplift the soul by its dispassionate beauty. The poet is a priest who should not take up a broom to sweep the streets, he is the Prophet to whom the angel appears in the desert. When he has finished his mission of bringing beauty, what do the opinions of the "Plebs" matter? (By "plebs" he meant, not the people, who have an instinct for beauty, but the vulgar, envious and frivolous members of high society.) But Pushkin had to pay dearly for his scorn of these "plebs": a group of callous evildoers set up in league against him, and used the innocent flirtations of his wife to load him with false illusions and anonymous letters: on January 27, 1837, he was provoked to challenge the French Baron d'Anthes to a duel; he was mortally wounded, and died two days later after bearing his terrible suffering with immense fortitude. Even after his death he was suspect: his body was taken to church at night, and transported to the monastery of the Holy Mountain near Mikhaylovskoye, where it now lies.

Other Romantics

Forgotten in the shadow of the greatest of Russian poets were many others, who in an earlier generation would have been more famous: Prince Viazemsky, Baron Delvig (a schoolfriend of Pushkin's), Yazykov and Benediktov all wrote elegantly. The Decembrists had a more serious attitude toward poetry: Kuchelbecker (another friend of Pushkin, who was exiled to Siberia) and Ryleev, one of the leaders of the insurrection, hanged in 1826, at the age of twenty-nine. The latter's political writings are full of vigor, but his *Doumys* (portraits drawn from Russian history) are lacking in variety and color: as he said himself, he was more "citizen" than poet. Venevitinov, who died at the age of twenty-two, was attracted by German philosophy, as was Baratynsky (1800–1844). This last, long unappreciated, was a great poet, one of the rare poet-philosophers of Russia. A sin he had committed in his youth weighed upon him for the rest of his life, and affected the development of his character. He was sent as a private soldier to Finland (he described the country in his *Eda*); his life was brightened by a happy marriage; and yet his pessimism (in which are traces of German influence, though it is profoundly sincere) did not leave him. He wrote of the futility of all human endeavor, of the absurdity of day following day, of a desire for nothingness. In thought as in form, he is a difficult poet, not destined for popularity. Polejaiev, whose fate resembled that of Baratynsky but who came to a more dismal end in alcohol and illness, exercised his talent in rebellion, but also composed songs for soldiers in the popular tradition (like those of the poet-partisan Davydov in 1812). Although it was the fashion of the day to imitate popular poetry, the works of Koltzov are anything but imitations; he was a man of the people, the son of an animal-dealer in Voroneje; from childhood on he used to go with his father on long journeys across the steppes, and he had to teach himself as well as he was able; when later he was feted in literary circles, he only felt more strongly the uncouthness of his family background; he wrote of joy and sadness, of work and holidays, of pastoral love, in simple language and melodious rhythms.

Since Pushkin cannot be confined within the framework of romanticism, the true romantic poet of Russia is Mikhail Yurevitch Lermontov, romantic in character, romantic in destiny. He was born in Moscow in 1814. Unhappy as a child, without a mother, he was surrounded with discord. He was extremely sensitive, and suffered from contact with his fellow students at boarding school, at university, and at the Military Academy at Petersburg where he was

preparing, after much hesitation, to enter the army; finding
no happiness in garrison life, he soon took refuge in writing
poetry. The death of Pushkin filled him with indignation
and grief, and in vehement verses he attacked the aristocracy
that had murdered him. He was sent in disgrace to the
Caucasus; his experiences in the high mountains made him
even more disgusted with the salons when, pardoned, he
returned to St. Petersburg, and he did not bother to conceal
this disgust. He made enemies, fought a duel and was again
banished to the Caucasus; there he took part in combats
that are recounted in his poem *Valerik*. In Piatigorsk he
met a former friend, a fatuous individual, whom he heaped
with sarcasm and provoked to a duel: Lermontov was killed
at the foot of the mountains in 1841, aged twenty-seven.

The relatively abundant work of this short life is filled
with bitter melancholy, arising from a somber and passionate character, a childhood surrounded with deceptions, and
fortified by the contagious *mal du siècle*. The unhappy poet
found himself portrayed in everything he read: in Pushkin's
early poems, in the French romantics (whom he held in high
esteem, contrary to Pushkin), in the works of Heine, but
above all in Byron; he discovered, with a sort of horror, such
a close affinity with the latter that he found it impossible
not to seem Byronic even when he was expressing his own
innermost thoughts. His lyrical poems echo his despondency,
his gnawing world-weariness. He did not revolt against
God, like Baratynsky and de Vigny: it was against man that
his anger was directed: man, who tears down all that is
great. Sworn to the hatred of man and to solitude, he took
refuge in nature, not to seek for friendship there, but because the spectacle of beauty drew him out of himself.

Lermontov loved especially the majestic Caucasian land-scape: he imagined an awe-inspiring dialogue between Mt. Elbrus and Mt. Kasbek, he described the furious race of the river Terek toward the Caspian, bearing as a gift the body of a beautiful young Cossack, and the wild gorges above which rose the castle of *Tamara,* the queen who sang at night to entice travelers to sensuality and death. He felt much closer to the proud mountain people than to the "civilized"; like them, he nursed a desperate need for free-dom. *The Novice* describes the sufferings of a Caucasian child captured by Russians and brought up in a monastery; he escapes, but loses his way in the mountains and is brought back dying to the monastery, still crying aloud his love for freedom. Another indomitable soul is *The Demon,* who seeks salvation in the love of a young Georgian girl and haunts her with disturbing visions, pursuing her even into the convent where she has taken refuge; the girl dies as a result of this love, but the Angels, like those in *Faust,* bear her soul away. This poem was begun very early in Lermontov's life and rewritten several times, the last time between 1838 and 1840; its theme echoes too closely Byron, Goethe and de Vigny. But one can forget this in the bril-liant descriptions and the impassioned voice of a soul that, sworn to evil, seeks vainly to free itself.

Quite different in inspiration is the short masterpiece *Song of the Tsar Vassilivitch, His Young Bodyguard, and the Bold Merchant Kalashnikov,* which brings to life the troubled period of the terrible Tsar in the tone and expres-sions of the *byliny* and as popular tradition conceived it.

As in *The Novice* and *The Demon,* there is much of

Lermontov himself in the play *The Masque;* the plot is melo-
dramatic, but the hero, who has something of Tchatski and
of Othello in him, stands out in tragic relief against the
worldly pettiness surrounding him. Much as he tried to avoid
it, there are also many aspects of Lermontov's character in
A Hero of Our Times, a collection made in 1840 of five
prose novels. Three of these, the most important, portray
one protagonist in different circumstances: Pechorin is as
blasé as Onegin, but more somber, more Byronic, full of
contradictions that he analyzes himself; he has long since
lost his youthful illusions of glory and love and become
henceforth selfish; he is dominating, capable of cool and
calculating malice, and yet still subject to passion and suffering. He is never satisfied, and can find happiness neither in
the love of a gentle, naïve Circassian girl, nor with the
women of his own environment, even though they too are
sincere. The portrayal of secondary figures such as the
cynical Dr. Verner, the good captain Maxim Maximytch
and the people of the mountains shows that Lermontov
could forget his own problems and write objectively. Had
he lived longer, he might, like Pushkin, have developed this
ability.

Apart from the works of Pushkin and Lermontov,
Russian prose writing lagged far behind poetry and produced nothing truly original during the romantic period.
Prince Vladimir Odoevski, whose imaginative novels have
a melancholy irony, was influenced by the philosophy of
Schelling and Wackenroder, the tales of Hoffmann, and the
novels of Jean-Paul. But Walter Scott was the author most
widely imitated: historical novels abounded, by the De-

cembrist Bestuyev (under the pseudonym of Marlinski), by Zagoskin, Lazhetchnikov and many others. The picturesque humor of the Ukrainian Narezhny influenced Gogol to some degree, but it was left to Gogol himself to guide the Russian novel along the paths of realism.

5 / *The Main Trends of Thought*

This is not the place to discuss the history of Russian thought. However, since the writer usually has the aim of being useful and not only of creating beauty, some indication should be given of the main trends of thought, which influenced the world of literature in Russia more than in any other country.

At the beginning of the century, Western ideas brought back by young officers who had been with the victorious armies of Alexander as far as Paris led to an awakening, and ended in the uprising of December, 1825. The failure of this attempt brought home the necessity of intellectual preparation, of some kind of doctrine. During the reign of Nicholas I there first appeared the Russian student who

stays up all night discussing metaphysics or politics between cigarettes and glasses of tea, as he is so often portrayed in the novels. Philosophy was introduced from Germany, and enthusiasm for Schelling, who had no political
doctrine, waned in favor of the Hegel cult; as in Germany,
some found in Hegel the justification of what is, and therefore of autocracy, and others the beginnings of socialist
theory. But Russia had to find her own application of this
philosophy: she had had in the past a particular type of
development, and the future seemed to hold a particular
destiny for her. Once more arose the problem that Peter I
had thought settled: should Russia learn from the ways of
Western Europe, and eventually surpass it, or should she
confine herself to her own resources? This was the question
that divided Westerners and Slavophils, both equally inspired by love of their country.

Westerners

In 1836 there appeared in the *Telescope* a *Philosophical
Letter* that caused a scandal. Its author was Chaadev (1794–
1856), a solitary aristocrat; he was considered mad and for
several years kept under medical observation. His theory
was developed in his other *Philosophical Letters*, which
were written in French and remained long unpublished. He
maintained that Russia was backward culturally because she
had received her civilization and, above all, her religion
from Byzantium, and had thus been separated from the advances made in the West; her only hope was to turn to
Roman Catholicism, and to follow the formative course of
other countries; only by doing this could she hope to draw

level; perhaps she would even surpass them, and find the answers to the problems that troubled them.

Before Vladimir Soloviev, Chaadev was alone in treating the question of a *rapprochement* with the West on a religious basis; the other Westerners sought social and political solutions to the problems. The great literary critic Belinsky (1811–1848) was a spirited soul who suddenly abandoned his reactionary Hegelian beliefs and went over to the opposite camp; he was poor and weakened by tuberculosis, and had a bitter struggle to earn his living in journalism (on the *Telescope* in Moscow, then after 1839 on the *Annals of the Fatherland* and the *Contemporary* in St. Petersburg), and above all to defend his beliefs. According to him, the task of literature was to spread the liberal ideas of the West on the one hand (he was a fervent admirer of George Sand), and on the other to expose the vices that were bringing Russia to shame. Although he was no partisan of "art for art's sake," he almost worshiped Pushkin, for Pushkin had turned from romantic idealism to realism. In Gogol's *Dead Souls* and *Revizor* he recognized with joy one of the most savage attacks on the Russian defects that had ever appeared, but was seized with indignation when he discovered in Gogol a mystical reactionary. He hailed in the talent of the young Dostoievsky and Turgenev the promise of great realistic works.

Chernyshevsky (1828–1889), who had chosen as a theme for his thesis *Aesthetic Relationship Between Art and Reality*, considered that beauty is only found in those works that reproduce faithfully that which exists, and which thus show the way to improvement. Like Chernyshevsky the son of a priest, and also representative of the new intellectual strata, was Dobroliubov (1836–1861), who succeeded him as critic on the *Contemporary;* he too saw in pure art only a pastime for young sentimentalists, and thought of literature as a vehicle for propaganda—it was in this light that he condemned Turgenev, Goncharov and Ostrovski. Pisarev (1841–1868) went even further: he objected to the pleasurable enjoyment of art, and longed for the day when art would no longer be necessary. The political intentions were easily distinguishable beneath this "nihilism," and the government sent Chernyshevsky to prison for two years (where he wrote his novel *What to Do?*) and to the mines in Siberia for seven years. Pisarev spent four years in the fortress of Peter-and-Paul, and Herzen was forced to go abroad in order to be able to develop his theories.

Herzen was born in 1812, the illegitimate son of a Russian aristocrat and a German girl, and died in Paris in 1870. In Moscow he studied science and the philosophy of Hegel and Saint-Simon, but was only just qualified as a civil servant when he was arrested and exiled to Viatka. Back in Moscow, he took the pseudonym of Iskander and wrote several articles and (*The Thieving Magpie*) a story against the feudal system. In 1846 he wrote the novel *Whose Fault?*, in condemnation of romanticism, of the selfish search for happiness in love. In 1847 he went abroad, but was disillusioned to find that the 1848 revolutions had changed nothing in the social structure, and that Berlin, Paris and London were still in the grips of the petit-bourgeois spirit. Only then, from afar, did he put his trust in Russia, the country that had no bourgeoisie, and that, in its peasant communities, the *mir,* had already partly realized the theory of socialism; if Russia could dare to by-pass the stages that had delayed the progress of the Western countries she would set an example to the whole world! Herzen's review, *The Bell*, which he had printed in London, was secretly distributed in Russia, and even penetrated as far as the Tsar's desk; the books in which he mingled memoirs and ideas under the title *My Past and Thoughts* had no less influence, though they were banned until 1917. Herzen was one of the first agitators to influence the thought of Russia from abroad; but at home he was already being outdistanced by others, by nihilists, or revolutionaries like Bakunin, who were advocating an immediate popular uprising.

Slavophiles

The opposite camp, the Slavophiles, also had its liberal partisans, who should not be dismissed as reactionaries without ideals (as they were by many of their opponents). They also desired reforms, and above all the abolition of the feudal system, but they sought to bring about these reforms in a purely Russian manner, and not in imitation of other countries. The feudal system was no primitive institution of ancient Russia: moreover, had not Russia set the example of a liberal social system in the *mirs*? (The two sides were united in admiration of the system of the *mirs*.) It was in Moscow, still less Europeanized than the new capital, that the Slavophiles established their doctrine: Constantine and Ivan Aksakov, Ivan and Peter Kireyevsky, and Alexis Khomiakov (1804–1860) were all deeply attached to orthodoxy, yet all aware, perhaps through Protestant influences, of its shortcomings, and eager to perfect and revive it. They criticized Catholicism for placing too much importance on dogma and reasoning; the Church of the East had better preserved the internal freedom of the mystics. To them, autocracy also was the protectress of true freedom; the Tsar, by assuming the responsibility of government, left his subjects at leisure to devote themselves to family life or to a life of meditation. But the picture could only be perfect if the ruler himself was perfect; it would have been difficult to realize in Russia under Nicholas I.

Khomiakov's anguish was doubled by the war in the Crimea: was his country not capable of fulfilling the task entrusted to it by God, because it had not understood it in time? It had to work to be worthy of this task, to break with the false reforms established by Peter the Great, to return to the old traditions, abolish the feudal system, strengthen the *mir* system and reorganize justice and administration.

In these aspects, the program of the Slavophiles was as daring as that of Herzen, and they were soon suspected by the government, which banned their review *The News of Moscow* (this came out in three editions: 1846, 1847 and 1851). The government also set up a doctrine using their motto "Orthodoxy, autocracy and national spirit"; but void of any liberal idealism, this was merely the catch-cry of reaction. Censorship increased, and every writer was suspected on principle; but persecution was never able to halt the progress of ideas.

Populists and Marxists

The feudal system was finally abolished, but the expected political reforms did not follow the social reform, which was anyway insufficient and left the peasants in a state of terrible poverty. The intellectuals, in a burst of enthusiasm, decided to "go to the people" in order to drag them out of their misery and ignorance; destructive nihilism gave way to a liberal "populism," avid for action. But opinions were divided on the choice of the way to be followed; should the masses first of all be educated, as Lavrov recommended in his *Historical Letters;* should they be roused to revolt at once, according to Bakunin's theory; or should the revolution take place without them, and if need be in spite of them, although they were to reap the benefits, as Tkatchev advocated? (It goes without saying that these three writers all made their pronouncements from abroad.) Many young men and women went into the countryside to teach, and were of course arrested at once; others formed terrorist groups; and yet others studied Marxist doctrine according to the theories of Plekhanov, Akselrod and later Lenin. Meanwhile the development of capitalism and industry and the appearance of a hitherto almost nonexistent working class, which was easier to teach and group than the peasantry, had changed the social structure of the country and given a new direction to the socialism that was to be led to victory by Lenin in 1917.

The Religious Philosophers

Political and social problems had not smothered the preoccupation with religion: in very different ways, this is at the basis of the works of Tolstoy and Dostoievsky; it had a decidedly Slavophile touch in the work of Constantin

Leontiev (1831–1891), who called for a universal theocracy with Russia at the head. Vladimir Soloviev (1853–1900), on the other hand, hoped for a union with Rome. The greatest Russian philosopher, and the first to be a metaphysician instead of a sociologist, Soloviev had considerable influence, not only on other philosophers—such as Chestov, Berdiaev and Losski—but also on poets (he himself was a poet). In the face of triumphant materialism he opened to them the doors of mystery, teaching them to see the external world only as the symbol of eternal Truth, and to seek this Truth, not through reason, but through intuition and faith. The brilliant and disturbing Vassily Rozanov (1856–1919) was also, in a sense, concerned with religion: he abandoned the Slavophiles, developed a hatred of Christian morality, and devoted himself to the mystical glorification of the flesh. Merezhkovsky tended to reconcile Soloviev with Rozanov, Christianity with paganism.

All these trends of thought are to be found in the literature of the nineteenth and twentieth centuries, and especially in the novel.

6 / The Novel in the Nineteenth Century

Gogol

However brilliant were the few novels of Pushkin and Lermontov, the real creator of the Russian novel was Nikolai Gogol. He was born in Sorochinets in the Ukraine in 1809; his father was interested in local customs, and wrote some comedies in Ukrainian that Gogol was later to put to use. He had a happy childhood in the country, and studied at the rather mediocre school at Niezhin, where his talent for acting was particularly noticed. This young southerner, with his thin face, long pointed nose and piercing eyes then set off for Petersburg, full of ambition: not only literary ambition, moreover, for he had dreams of playing a major role in the destiny of his country. Like many Ukrainians, he was at once a humorist and a dreamer, imaginative and realistic, gifted with observation and imitation. But he was also introspective, irritable and unsentimental, which are rare qualities in that race; there were to be no women in his life, and apart from descriptions of a few old women, there are no successful female characters in his work. He was a believer, almost a mystic; at an early age he told his mother that God had great designs for him. The modest job offered him could not possibly satisfy his needs; he thought of becoming an actor, then entered the literary world with a verse idyll in imitation of Voss, *Hans Kuchelgarten;* as soon as the first criticism appeared, he destroyed it and fled abroad. But hardly had he arrived in Lubeck than he returned. Stimulated by the success of popular legends, of local color in literature, and in particular of all things Ukrainian, he wrote his *Evenings at a Farm Near Dikanka* (1831–1832), which earned him at once the glory of which he had already despaired, access to literary circles, and the approval and friendship of Pushkin. Perhaps this evocation of the Ukraine is not entirely authentic, with its mixture of childhood memories and "tales of Hoffmann," but it is overflowing with life, with racy humor and fantasy. There are some irresistibly comic effects in *The Fair at Sorochinets,* and macabre passages in *Midsummer's Eve;* already there are realistic caricatures and beautiful romantic descriptions, without precise details but lyrical and rich in imagery. Encouraged by his success, Gogol went back to the Ukraine to refresh his memories; he returned disillusioned, but full of ideas for his new collection *Mirgorod* and for other stories. There is still an element of fantasy in *Viy*, but the amusing *Ivan Ivanovich and Ivan Nikiforovich* is realistic and sparkles with irony; in *Old-World Landowners* the irony is tempered with emotion; the dust-to-dust life of the old household savors of a profound tenderness. *Taras Bulba* is a romantic though historically inexact evocation of the heroic past of the Ukraine; it is vivid and colorful, with dazzling descriptions of the steppes in flower and of the camp of the Zaporogs.

This excursion into history gave Gogol the illusion that he had a calling in the field: without any education in the subject, he applied for and obtained the chair of Professor of History at Petersburg University; he was a resounding failure there and returned to literature. He began by describing the life of Petersburg, using the technique that had earned him so much success in his stories of the Ukraine. But since the capital was a less poetic subject, realism was more pronounced in *The Nevsky Prospect, The Memoirs of a Madman*, and particularly in the wonderful *Greatcoat*, a sad and simple tale of a humble office-worker whose new coat, acquired after years of dreaming and saving, is stolen the first night he wears it. The story's fantasy ending follows a description of the day-to-day life of the humiliated old man, a description that prompted Dostoievsky to say that all the novels of Russia were born of Gogol's *The Greatcoat;* there is a note of pity that foreshadows Dostoievsky himself, when a young official, watching the unfortunate Akaki Akakievitch being ridiculed by those around him, suddenly thinks, "This man is my brother."

His gift of observation, his comic sense, the vivacity of his dialogue, meant that Gogol was destined to succeed in the theatre. The success of *Revizor*, however, put him in an acutely embarrassing situation: faced with the indignation of the reactionaries and the enthusiasm of the liberals, he protested sincerely but in vain that he had not in any way wished to criticize the institutions of his country. To escape the controversy aroused by his play, in order to be able to work in peace, and also to satisfy the need of privacy that had first prompted his escape to Lubeck and thenceforth never left him, he left Russia in 1848 and for twelve years led a wandering life. He traveled through Germany, France—which he detested for its atheistic liberalism—and Italy, which he loved for its sun and the religious atmosphere of Rome. His constant companion was the work he had started in 1835, the great work of his life, *Dead Souls;* he could say that this was the story of his own soul. The first part appeared in 1842 under the title of *The Adventures of Chichikov, or Dead Souls.* The theme, suggested by Pushkin, is based on an incident that had appeared in a newspaper: a swindler considers buying "dead souls," or serfs who have died after the last census, and for whom the landowners are still paying taxes; these landowners will be only too happy to sell him at a high price the titles to property that will serve him as guarantees for bank loans. Chichikov sets off through the countryside on his singular mission in his swift brichka, which quickly became a legend. He is made to inspire confidence; he is neither young nor old, plump and spruce, blessed with a robust appetite and a laughing disposition, able to laugh at a peasant's joke or appear quite at ease in the drawing room of the governor. No one is interested in his past record, and the reader is only enlightened as to their dubious nature at the end of the volume; but is Chichikov in fact any less honest than the provincial civil servants or the country landowners with whom he conducts his shady dealings? The reader is led through a whole gallery of unforgettable portraits: the idle, mildly sentimental nobleman, the brutish neighbor who avidly defends his interests, the sly, shallow old woman, the swaggering, deceitful prodigal, the sordid and tragic miser. Our "commercial traveler" skillfully varies his tactics according to the character of each one, and the ensuing dialogue is racily different each time; not one is prompted by honesty to resist the advantageous yet suspect offer; they are all tempted by the prospect of material profit; these living people are all dead souls. This symbolism was far from Gogol's thoughts when at the beginning of the book he wrote to Pushkin "This will be most amusing." But when Pushkin read the first few chapters he exclaimed: "My God, how sad our Russia is," and the liberals and conservatives alike, as in the case of *Revizor,* agreed that this merry story was a heartbreaking picture of the real Russia. How was it possible to conceive that the author of a work which implied such a fierce condemnation of the feudal system could be a partisan of it, that he had only thought to convey the comedy of the situation and some character studies, but that his gift for caricature and uncompromisingly lucid observation had in spite of himself given his work a slant that he had not foreseen? This misunderstanding was one of the causes of a tragedy that was to shake Gogol to the soul, a tragedy already evident in the first, realistic part of the story, where there are short lyrical outbursts extolling his faith in the Russian people, in the future of a Russia that, like a fiery

troika, would gallop past a stupefied Europe. He was accused of insulting his country, yet during his voluntary exile
his adoration of Russia grew: if the first part of his poem
was, like Dante's, an Inferno, then it would be followed by
Purgatory, in which Chichikov would become a reformed
man, and a Paradise in which he would reveal to the world
all the splendid attributes of the Russian soul. But although
he could capture the ridiculous and the vicious, Gogol was
incapable of creating a virtuous character who was also con-
vincing; he was conscious of this and irritated by it. Between 1843 and 1845 he wrote the second part of *Dead
Souls,* destroyed it and started it again (in the few chapters
that have been preserved in draft, the only good parts are
those that are intensely critical). Not realizing that the diffi-
culty lay in the nature of his talent, he thought his own soul
must be unworthy: he was too imperfect to create perfect
beings. Terrified by the God-given mission to lead his
people, in which he was bound to fail, he felt compelled to
confess in public, to wail out his need of help. In 1846 he
published his *Selected Passages From a Correspondence
With Friends,* which created a scandal: it betrayed Gogol's
true convictions, it revealed him as a conservative and a
mystic, and it adjured Russia in the tones of a prophet to
renew herself and help him also to renew himself. He went
to the Holy Land in the hope of finding inspiration, but
the journey only served to bring home to him "the dryness
in my heart." He suddenly decided to return to Russia, in
order to be able to see and portray it better; in Moscow, he
was disturbed by a monk who admonished him for the
vanity of his literary ambitions. The artist and the ascetic
struggled within him; on February 12, 1852, he set fire to

all that he had written of the second part of *Dead Souls;*
exhausted after his sacrifice and his fasting, he died a few
days later.

From Gogol to Dostoievsky

Dead Souls established for some time to come the characteristics of the Russian novel: realistic above all else, it
set out to portray individuals, and particularly the milieu
they represented. This resulted in the writer taking sides,
willingly or unwillingly (as in the case of Gogol), or at least
appearing to the critic to take sides, in political and social
issues. There were no more works in which the "opinions"
were not rooted out.

If there was an opinion to be found in the work of
Sergei Aksakov (1791–1859), the friend of Gogol and the
father of the two Slavophiles, it was a conservative one,
full of a tender respect for the past. This excellent man, who
loved nature and animals, began writing in his old age, with
his *Memoirs of a Fisherman* and *Memoirs of a Hunter;* he
then applied his gifts of observation to human beings in
A Family Chronicle and *Years of Childhood of Bagrov-
Grandson,* which depicted his family background with
charming simplicity.

Goncharov and Turgenev were also peaceable men, devoted to their art; but by virtue of their gift for bringing to
life whatever they saw, both disturbed people more than
they intended.

Goncharov was born in Simbirsk in 1812; he grew up
on one of the wealthy, somnolent properties that he de-

scribed in his works, where the meals were conducted with ceremony and where all the days were alike, and he never lost his love of peace and comfort. His career as a civil servant, and as a liberal-minded censor, only brought with it one unexpected event: he took part in the long periplus of the frigate *Pallada,* and his account of the journey round Africa and Asia is filled with light-hearted and amusing observations. He died a bachelor in 1891; he had no strong religious or political convictions and though he witnessed one of the great events of his time, the abolition of the feudal system, he remained unmoved by it. His only passion was for literature, and he was happiest spending long hours putting the finishing touches to his three novels: *A Common Story* (1847), *Oblomov* (1859) and *The Ravine* (1859), in which he set down the observations on himself and his surroundings that he had stored up day by day.

A Common Story is about a young man who, like one of Balzac's heroes and, no doubt, the author himself, arrives in the capital filled with notions of a high position, literary glory and a great love affair, but is forced by deception after deception to see and accept himself for what he really is: an egoist and a failure.

Certain aspects of Aduyev's character are echoed in that of *Oblomov,* but the hero of the latter is more generous by nature and has real talents; he wants to escape the lure of the family seat, to learn, to do something, but his apathy proves too strong: he spends his time lounging on his couch dreaming of what he will do one day. An energetic friend and a valiant woman try to save him, but Oblomov is incapable of sustaining his efforts toward regeneration, and finally sinks forever into lassitude. In Oblomov, Goncharov managed to create one of the most celebrated character types in the Russian novel, and through him denounce the great national failing: the oriental apathy that had paralyzed so many energetic liberal movements; in fact, the name that Oblomov, with unhappy insight, himself created—"Oblomovtchina"—is still used for this particular failing.

In *The Ravine*, the tediousness of the intrigue is not recompensed as it is in the first two novels by the force of the psychological insight: Goncharov was unable to give life to a character who had nothing of himself. And this is where Turgenev excelled him.

There was something of Oblomov in Ivan Turgenev, as there was in Goncharov, but in the case of Turgenev it vanished when there was a work of art to be created. Alphonse Daudet called him "the body of a cyclops with the soul of a woman."

He was born in 1818 at Orel of a family with distant Tartar origins. His father was weak, his mother a harsh woman whose severe treatment of the serfs filled him with horror of the feudal system; he was brought up on the wealthy property at Spaskoye, and always retained his childhood love of nature and poetry. He studied philosophy in Russia and then in Berlin, and met liberal-minded young people. When he returned to Petersburg, he frequented the salons, wrote some verses and a few short plays; then, in 1847, he wrote *Khor and Kalynich*, the first of his *Sportsman's Sketches*, soon after he had met and fallen in love with the actress Pauline Viardot, then on tour in Russia. This love, however, was destined to be no more than friendship, and from then on the lonely bachelor lived with the Viardots, who gave him the illusion of a family life; he followed them across Europe (returning each summer to Spaskoye), settled with them in Baden in 1864, and from 1871 on in Paris; there he frequented the Magny restaurant, and became the friend of the Goncourts, de Maupassant, Alphonse Daudet, George Sand and above all of Flaubert. His conversation was full of charm, and he did a good deal to promote in Paris a love of Russia and its literature. But he suffered from having lost contact with his country, and from the misunderstandings that arose between him and the younger generation in Russia. He died at Bougival in 1883, after long months of suffering during which, faithful to his art to the end, he composed his last *Poems in Prose*.

After the great success of *A Sportsman's Sketches* in 1852, Turgenev devoted himself entirely to his work. Since Gogol, rustic literature had been continually popular in Russia, and was now the fashion throughout Europe (George Sand's *La Mare au Diable* was written a year before *Khor and Kalynich*): Vladimir Dahl had put his knowledge of the patois to good use in this genre, and Grigorovitch (1822–1899) had published in 1846 *The Village* and in 1847 *The Misfortunes of Antony*, following *The Fisherman* and *The Emigrants*—tableaux of rustic manners that were hailed with enthusiasm by Belinsky, who was blind to the sentimental and conventional elements in them; no rustic literature, Russian or not, ever equaled the poetic simplicity of *A Sportsman's Sketches*.

This Sportsman—who is Turgenev himself—treks across fields and woods, meets the peasants, goes to a fair and a burial, seeks shelter at a small country seat or an izba: the whole of the Russian countryside unfolds before us, and the strongest protest is silently made against the feudal system. Turgenev prized as his main claim to glory the effect of his book on public opinion and on the Tsar himself, although he provoked no argument; while not attempting to minimize the faults of the mujiks, he did show their true intelligence, their good sense, the richness of their thoughts and feelings, and the cruelty of their slavery. It was not that the lords who whipped them, enforced marriage upon them, and deported them at whim were monsters, but that the feudal system, the secular condition of seigneurial comfort, had deadened in their masters any sense of the brotherhood of man.

Turgenev had the gift of creating in a few lines unforgettable, typical characters of nobleman or peasant, each with his own language; the story, sometimes funny, more often melancholy, is punctuated with descriptive passages in which the evocative power of the poet is linked with the huntsman's detailed knowledge of plants and animals; it conjures up heavy heat in the undergrowth, misty autumn mornings, the splendor of the sunrises and sunsets over the gentle undulation of the plain, a starry night above the Bezhin Meadow, when the children who keep watch over the horses sense that the evil spirits are prowling around them.

The short stories were succeeded by a series of great novels. In 1856 *Rudin* enlarged upon the Russian Hamlet-type character who had already appeared in the *Sketches* and who was to reappear in various guises in all the subsequent works of Turgenev: the man of intelligence and generosity, but lacking in will power, incapable of action and even of real passion. Quite different are Turgenev's young women: depicted so exquisitely, some all tenderness, some all energy, they let nothing get in their way once they have given their love. Another theme, introduced in this first novel, and used frequently in later works, is the opposition of two generations: the unidealistic fathers who lead a traditional life in their country residences, and the sons, alienated from their milieu by foreign culture, who become fuddled with ideas and ineffectual words.

A Nest of Gentlefolk (1859) is merely a charming and old-fashioned tale of unhappy love, but in *On the Eve* (1860) Turgenev returned to his obsessional search for the energetic man who was to be essential in the coming new era (the abolition of the feudal system was near at hand); he found him neither in the frivolous and attractive artist, nor in the timid intellectual, but in the character of the Bulgarian Insarov, weak in body but strong in spirit, who dedicates himself to the liberation of his country and dies before he has even started his task; he is beloved of the passionate Helen, who had been suffocating in an atmosphere of selfishness. Was it therefore impossible to find in Russia a man at once strong and daring? In *Fathers and Sons* (1861) Turgenev gave his answer, to the discontent of the youth of Russia. As always he avoided taking sides: aristocratic parents are granted to have refinement of habit and sentiment, and a taste for beauty; humble parents have the solid religious and moral traditions of old Russia. As for the children, we have Arcade, another weak young man, though with an excellent heart; once he gets over his youthful aspirations he will carry on peacefully as his father has done. But the "nihilist" Bazarov is cast in another mold; sweeping aside the past, he is insolent, intransigent, materialistic in philosophy and in love; he submits everything to scientific experiment, denying art and poetry; it is evident that in politics he would call for a total revolution. But strong as he is, he is conquered by life: he is shattered by love, and he dies of a dreadful disease.

The book aroused an unprecedented reaction among the intellectual youth, who vehemently criticized the author for the pessimistic note of the ending and wrongly accused him of taking sides against Bazarov. In fact, affection for the past, curiosity for the future, anguish for his own times, all mingled in Turgenev's soul as in this novel, which was both a chronicle of the period and a work of art, classical in its objectivity.

Discouraged by the general lack of understanding, Turgenev attacked reactionaries and liberals, Slavophiles and Westerners, fathers and sons alike, in *Smoke* (1867), a powerful and picturesque depiction of the Russian community of Baden, with its endless sterile discussions. It was all so much smoke, like everything Russian, like everything in life. However, the book ends on a happier note with a word of advice: to work quietly in the place where one can be of use. *Virgin Soil* (1876) comes to the same conclusion, but it is a weaker work, revealing too clearly how little the author knew about the revolutionary younger generation.

Meanwhile Turgenev had not been neglecting the short story, in which his stylistic and rhythmic qualities were finding their fullest expression. In 1873 he added *Living Relics* to the *Sportsman's Sketches*. Then he restricted himself to very short works, the *Poems in Prose,* which outlined in a few words his disillusioned philosophy: men thrash about in vain, while nature looks on, indifferent, eternal; all that is left to man, once he has understood the vanity of his aspirations, is to devote himself humbly to a useful task, or to take refuge in the serenity of art.

To this serenity of the artist, which was both Turgenev's and Pushkin's, his contemporaries preferred battle: they took sides, and the public, often disconcerted by Turgenev's objective attitude, classed them simply as progressive or reactionary. After the abolition of the feudal system, the liberals still had many things to grumble about: the poverty of the peasants, the corruption of businessmen and officials, the absence of any political reform, all provided food for discontent to the "accusers."

Pride of place among the latter must be given to Saltykov (1826–1889), who wrote at first under the pseudonym of Schedrin. He was a nobleman who, apart from a few years in disgrace at Viatka, led quite a fine career as a civil servant until 1868, when he resigned in order to join Nekrasov in running *Annals of the Fatherland*. He brought back from Viatka his *Provincial Sketches,* which he followed with *Satires in Prose, Innocent Tales, The History of a Town, The Golovlev Family* (1880), *Gentlemen of Tashkent, Diary of a Provincial, Milords and Ladies Pompadour,* and others. His biting, caustic satire, which has been compared to that of Swift, was directed at all classes of society, only showing some degree of indulgence toward the peasants. *The Golovlev Family* paints a somber picture of a noble family weighed down by a long tradition of vice and idleness, and given the final blow by the abolition of the feudal system. There is a striking portrayal of a greedy and vicious old woman, whose whole life has been dominated by the idea of family, in the sense that she has kept her children round her, but with no concern for the children themselves: more sinister still is the hypocrite Yuduchka, her youngest son, a degenerate who brings about the final collapse of the family.

But, side by side with these misfits, the novels of Saltykov present a number of men who have been able to adapt themselves only too well to the new conditions and to profit from them: the civil service offered officials of all grades opportunities to get rich, above all in the distant provinces, which were more or less colonies where the local inhabitants were at their mercy (*Gentlemen of Tashkent*); if the fortune-seeker was very successful, he developed into a Pompadour in the shape of a provincial governor or an unscrupulous minister. For was not the whole of Russia a happy land of Tashkent, where "the sheep were ready to be fleeced at any time of year"? *The History of a Town* (the town of Glupov) is the history of Russia, with the Tsars disguised as governors and the people resigned to everything. This illusive technique, together with a rough and obscure style, makes Saltykov difficult for modern Russians to understand; his work has aged more than others, because he was rarely able to do anything more than depict the mores of an epoch, but as a document of that epoch his work is unparalleled. Full of allusions also is the novel of Reshetnikov, *The People of Podlipnoye* (1864), a picture of the hard life of the peasants in the region of the Kama that implies the material and moral poverty of the whole of Russia. *What to Do?*, by Chernyshevsky (1864), immensely successful when it came out, today appears artificial, with its too-perfect student couple who are devoured by the sacrificial spirit, and its gentleman Tolstoyan-before-Tolstoy who becomes a wagoner and tracker on the Volga.

The conservative writers were no less realistic, but they drew different conclusions. Pisemsky (1820–1881) had united the pleas of both right and left in his *Thousand Souls,* the story of an adventurer even more unscrupulous than Chichikov; in *Troubled Seas,* however, he shows Russian society thrown into confusion by the abolition of the feudal system, and presents himself as decidedly reactionary.

The great talent of Leskov (1831–1895) remained long undiscovered because of his own inclinations; however, Gorky made a great issue of it. He was too poor to be able to study, and he made his living in commerce, traveling through Russia. In 1862 he wrote an article directed against the revolutionary students, which aroused their hatred; this was increased by his novels *No Way Out* and *At Daggers Drawn,* which were directed against socialism and full of unpleasant personal allusions. Happily these aggressive works do not constitute the whole of Leskov's writings. His *Cathedral Folk* (1872) gives a picture of ecclesiastics unique in Russian literature: it offers many noble figures of monks, but is only too ready to ridicule priests; the hero, Tuberosov, whose soul burns with faith and charity, has to battle against both the hostility of the intellectuals and the narrow-mindedness of his superiors, and he is defeated. Other works depict other circles that Leskov knew from first-hand experience: the provincial merchants in *A Lady Macbeth of Mtsensk District,* and the Old Believers in *The Sealed Angel.* These short works display a good deal of artistic talent in their carefully chiseled language.

Melnikov (1819–1883), whose pen name was Pechersky, resembles Leskov in his choice of themes, but is inferior to him both as a man and as a writer. He was a schoolmaster at Perm and Nijni-Novgorod, and was interested in local customs, particularly those of the Old Believers, who were numerous on the far side of the Volga; he was accused of having betrayed their confidence in order to furnish the administration—which he joined after giving up his teaching post—with weapons against them. He wrote two long novels about them: *In the Forests* (1872) and *In the Mountains* (1875–1880), describing their customs—which had not changed since the Schism—their life in the villages and monasteries hidden in the depths of the woods, the sometimes mystic form of their faith—which was deprived of priests—their honest and hardworking nature, and their narrow-mindedness and the excessive severity of their family discipline. These highly colorful tableaux are lacking in any warmth to move the reader.

Dostoievsky

The conservatives have claimed Dostoievsky as one of their own; in fact, his professed beliefs do correspond to their ideas, but as if in spite of himself, his genius has escaped all attempts to define him, and his work has fallen to the common inheritance of mankind.

Fedor Mikhaylovich Dostoievsky, born in Moscow in 1821, was the son of a severe, avaricious and pious doctor of the lower ranks of the nobility. With very little fortune—in contrast with most of the Russian writers—he grew up in the city, and it is in the city that his novels are set. The deaths of his mother and of Pushkin were the great tragedies of his early years. When he was seventeen, studying subjects that he disliked at the Military Engineers' School in Petersburg, his father was murdered by the peasants to whom he had been a very hard master. Fedor Mikhaylovich, who had been prone to fits of depression since childhood, suffered his first epileptic attack on hearing the news. He stayed in the army only a year, and then decided to take up writing. In 1844 his first novel, *Poor Folk,* which was much influenced by Gogol's *Greatcoat,* received the enthusiastic approval of Belinsky and Nekrasov. But the works that followed were too hastily written. Attracted by liberal ideas that he was later to renounce, he joined the fairly harmless Petrashevsky group, was arrested with them in 1849, and condemned to death. The tense minutes when he stood before the firing squad facing imminent death are recalled several times in his books.

The imperial pardon was deferred by a cruel trick on the part of the authorities, and was only revealed at the last minute; it accorded him a partial reprieve, and he was sent to the prison of Omsk. What the four years that he spent there were like can be gathered from *The House of the Dead,* although neither in this book nor at any time in his life did he complain; he contented himself with describing the horrible life of the prisoners, and with seeking in these fallen men sparks of divine grace. His health was ruined when he came out of the prison. He served as a private soldier for some time in Semipalatinsk, then his rank of officer and his nobility were restored to him, but he was not allowed back in Russia until 1859. In Siberia he had married an ailing and temperamental widow, Maria Isayeva. As soon as he returned, his glory was assured by the appearance of *The House of the Dead* and *The Humiliated and Insulted;* soon afterward, with his brother Michael, he founded a review, *Vremya* ("The Time"), which was shortly banned. In 1862 he made his first journey to the West, and in 1863 he set off again to follow the student Apollinaria Suslova to Paris; she had deceived him even before he arrived. They did, however, travel around Germany together, after which he returned to Petersburg, where he had to cope with all kinds of troubles: his wife and his brother both died, and left him debts and a family to look after. Then he was really forced to work, he who had always been paid in advance for work barely started, and had then worked furiously, haunted by the approach of the deadline. To speed up his work, he hired a young typist, Anna Snitkin, whom he married in 1867; she admired him without understanding him, and enveloped him in a tight web of tenderness and devotion. They spent several years in Germany and Switzerland, years filled with sadness, which was aggravated by a passion for gambling that drew Dostoievsky irresistibly toward the roulette table. In 1871, with their two surviving children, they settled in Petersburg, and their financial situation improved slightly when Madame Dostoievsky decided to edit her husband's work herself. In order to give more direct expression to his political and religious convictions (which were one and the same) than was afforded him by the novel, Dostoievsky published periodically *An Author's Diary;* he emerged from his solitude in 1880 to give an address at the unveiling of the Pushkin memorial that earned him enthusiastic ovations. But he was already worn out by the hardship of his youth, his excessive work and his illnesses—besides epilepsy he had emphysema—and in January, 1881, he was confined to bed with a pulmonary hemorrhage, and died, in the rites of the Church.

The great novels of Dostoievsky—*Crime and Punishment* (1866), *The Gambler* (1868), *The Idiot* (1868), *The Eternal Husband* (1869), *The Possessed* ("The Devils," 1871), *The Adolescent* (1875), *The Brothers Karamazov* (an unfinished work of which the first two volumes appeared in 1877)—all merit a detailed study, but we can only try here to convey their essential aspects.

The central plot, which is comparatively simple, nearly always concerns a crime. *Crime and Punishment* portrays a young and ambitious student who murders an old woman in order to rob her, and who eventually gives himself up. *The Idiot* is a basically good man who, between the woman he loves and a woman who needs to be saved, chooses to marry the latter; she rejects his sacrifice, and goes off with another man who kills her. *The Possessed* reveals a socialist conspiracy: one of the members of the party is suspected of treason and is murdered. *The Brothers Karamazov* describes a sensational miscarriage of justice. These works have elements of the serial novel, even of the detective story: the trick of concealing the secrets of one or more of the characters until the end, the improbable meetings between characters at unexpected moments and in unexpected places, the many episodes that accelerate the action, the accumulation of violent deaths, particularly in *The Possessed,* and the large number of secondary plots.

Dostoievsky had such a strong creative force that characters seem to spring up spontaneously, and have to be given places. He sees them, and makes us see them, through a few characteristics that impose themselves upon the memory—such as old Karamazov's Adam's apple. There are only a few descriptive passages, and these nearly all townscapes and interiors; they are less described than suggested, and are always directly relevant to a state of mind, for it was man's mind that fascinated Dostoievsky. He was much more objective than Tolstoy, and only a few scattered traits of his own character come through in his creations, but he lives with them each minute of their lives, and follows their every step; one of his innovations of technique, which has greatly influenced the development of the modern novel, is the interest with which he examined his characters at times and in situations that have nothing to do with the story, and he devoted much space to the study of the subconscious, of the strange forces that can lead men to make unexpected decisions—especially the passionate and nervous types he preferred to portray, many of whom are almost pathological cases: Prince Myshkin and Smerdiakov are both epileptic, one a saint, the other a monster. Many of them have visions, terrifying ones for the sinful, comforting for Alyosha Karamazov. Dostoievsky was not interested in the happy medium—he caricatured the heroes of Turgenev, and Turgenev himself in *The Possessed*—but in people who were capable of criminal or sublime acts; he studied them scientifically, confronting them with crime and with love, and he distinguished three types: the man of thought, ruled by his intelligence; the man of passion, ruled by the flesh, and finally, the simple and pure man.

Dostoievsky's obsession with crime has been attributed to a Freudian regression or a secret sin, but it is more likely that the time he spent in prison brought home to him the problem of the criminal's relationship with his act (he noticed habitual absence of remorse), the genesis of the crime, and its repercussions on the mind. Raskolnikov, the student in *Crime and Punishment,* is a man of thought who is led by a process of reasoning to commit murder: the extinction of a harmful creature, an old woman pawnbroker, to insure a fruitful life to the exceptionally gifted creature he felt himself to be, could not possibly constitute a crime: a Newton, a Napoleon has no right to die. But Raskolnikov is guided by intelligence, not will power: crushed by the secret he has to bear, he is unable to reap the profits of his crime. It is not remorse, however, that leads him to give himself up: he continues to regard as irrefutable the process of reasoning that has guided him, but at the same time despises his weakness. Only much later, in prison, and close to the humble Sonya, does he understand the law of love and pity that he has transgressed. Ivan Karamazov is also highly intelligent and believes that everything is permissible, but he is even less capable of action than Raskolnikov: it is Smerdiakov who, convinced by his lessons, kills old Karamazov, but Ivan knows that he is the one responsible.

Each novel balances the intellectual with a creature of the flesh who cannot resist his impure passions; in *Crime and Punishment* there is Svidrigaylov, in *The Idiot* Rogozhin, and in *The Brothers Karamazov* both Dmitri (whose obsession with sensual pleasure is all the more tragic because his is a generous nature), and also, to the worst abject degree, old Karamazov. Moreover, there is an instinct of base sensuality in all men, and even the angelic Alyosha knows that there is Karamazov blood in him, and does not despise his father. Pure creatures, who belong to the kingdom of the Madonna rather than to the kingdom of Sodom, are too humble to consider themselves superior to the impure, to the criminal; they have only a brother-love for them; while the intellectuals and the sensual are equally egotistical, the pure are all love; they love men because they believe in God. They are children, or women: Sonya, who has become a prostitute through her devotion to her family, who follows Raskolnikov to prison; Dasha, ready to devote herself to Stavrogin, and Grushenka to Dmitri; and they are men as well: Prince Myshkin, the "idiot" who knows in his heart what no intellectual could ever deduce by reason, Father Zosima and the sweet-natured Alyosha Karamazov. The law of love that they incarnate dominates the religious and political thought of Dostoievsky.

The importance given in the novels to dialogue and to discussions of ideas that interrupt the action detracts from the artistic perfection, but gives it profundity: the reader becomes aware of a duality in the mind of the author, of doubts that a hidden force obliged him to formulate and to which his reason tried to find the answers. After his return from Siberia he declared himself in all sincerity to be a partisan of autocracy, and in *The Possessed* he made a violent attack on socialism. But some vestiges of the energy of his youth are still discernible; perhaps, when confronted with the lure of revolution, he was sheltering behind autocracy, just as when assailed by religious doubts he took shelter behind orthodoxy. The two concepts were linked in his mind; confusing socialism with atheism, he criticized it for thinking only of the material life and for destroying the freedom of the individual. Orthodoxy for him was a free religion, as opposed to Catholicism, a religion of dogma and hierarchy that, in spite of the fact that Christ had come to free men, had enslaved them. To be Russian was to be Orthodox. The Russian people, who carried God within them, "would some day have something new to tell the world," and Dostoievsky chose orthodoxy so as to be one with his people; he was tempted to deny it, to affirm his total liberty as a superman by killing himself, like Kirilov in *The Possessed*, but he was saved, like Chatov in the same book, because he believed in Russia; like Alyosha, he "wanted to believe" in God, and his soul, eternally in torment, felt from afar the serenity of Father Zosima, the ecstasy of Alyosha. This peace could only be conquered by the love of God and man, by the acceptance of suffering, even though unmerited, as the only way to being reborn. Unhappiness had for him a sacred character. As long as men did not understand these truths, which were the message from Russia to the whole world, then they would go on fighting each other in contradiction, in the temptations of the flesh and of the spirit; they would continue to be drawn by crime, by the forces of evil; it is from this tortured and chaotic world that the novels of Dostoievsky bring their disturbing images.

Tolstoy

Dostoievsky and Tolstoy, both profoundly Russian, had in common a burning need to find the redeeming Truth and announce it to the world, but it would be impossible to find two more different temperaments and talents. Dostoievsky's life was marked by terrible trials, while Tolstoy's was apparently peaceful; Dostoievsky worked feverishly, Tolstoy at leisure; Dostoievsky was a sick man, excessively impressionable, while Tolstoy was overflowing with vigor; one was prone to uneasy cross-currents of emotion and irrational impulses, while the other was logical and tenacious; Dostoievsky was a mystic in spite of his doubts, Tolstoy a logician in spite of his religious crises; Dostoievsky wanted to conserve, Tolstoy to destroy. Both filled their novels with ideas, but the philosophy of Dostoievsky limited itself to a few very simple ideas that varied during his life and that he affirmed with total conviction each time. Foreigners have tended too much to see Russia through the eyes of Dostoievsky, and are only just beginning to recognize in her the forceful vitality and logical perseverance of Tolstoy.

The life and work of Tolstoy are divided into a series of wide successive stages in which he stopped whenever he found an explanation of life that would allow him to live and create; after each of these halts came a period of disturbance and seeking, which would take him to the next level.

Count Leo Nikolayevich Tolstoy was born on August 28, 1828, in Yasnaya Polyana, in the province of Tula. His paternal ancestors had long been involved in the history of Russia—and also in some scandalous affairs; but nobler and richer was the family of his mother, the princess Volkonsky, who died when he was two years old. His father died when Leo was nine, and he was brought up by aunts. At Kazan University, he studied oriental languages and law for a while, but at the age of nineteen he suddenly abandoned his studies and devoted himself to developing his land and seeing to the happiness of his serfs. He was soon discouraged, and after leading a life of pleasure for some time in Petersburg, he went off to the Caucasus to join one of his brothers, signed on in the army, and became an officer.

He had always read a lot, and admired Pushkin, Gogol, Montesquieu and particularly Rousseau, whose enormous influence he acknowledged; and from an early age he entertained hopes of writing. In the Caucasus he composed *Childhood*, which was published in 1852; this was not a collection of authentic memories, but like all his works, a mixture of fact and fiction, of real people and imaginary characters; but in any case the child at the center of the work is himself, with his susceptibilities, his joys and his chagrins. Already in the succession of scenes—a day in the country, the journey, a day in Moscow—Tolstoy had attained perfect visual evocation. The second and third parts of the work—*Boyhood* and *Youth*—were written unwillingly, without spontaneity; other aspects of life were already drawing him.

The Caucasus had a profound impression on this disciple of Rousseau, and provided the first answer to the question he was already asking: what is the point of life? In a long novel that he was planning, but that stayed at the stage of a story, *The Cossacks*, this reply is given to the young sophisticate by Uncle Yerochka, a man of nature who loves trees and plants and yet hunts remorselessly because that is one of nature's laws: "God made everything for man's delight. . . . There is no such thing as sin."

This love of life gained strength from the contact with death that was ever present with the soldier; during the

Crimean War, while his regiment was besieged at Sevastopol, Tolstoy was struck by the simple way in which the
ordinary man, understanding nothing of war, suffered and
died; this simplicity makes his accounts of *Sevastopol* very
striking. But in his own more complex soul, the horrors of
the siege shook his faith in the laws of nature, and he
went back to Petersburg not knowing where to turn next.
However, soon he began to hope that progress would render
man peaceful and good; these hopes suffered cruel blows
during a journey abroad, to countries more "civilized" than
Russia but nevertheless cruel (he was present at an execu-
tion in Paris), but he still tried to contribute to progress.
He started a school in Yasnaya Polyana, and adapted books
to be read by the people. At the same time, he tried to live
a simple family life: in 1862 he married Sophie Behrs; he
was thirty-four, she eighteen, a serious, passionate and
irritable girl. For many years they lived happily, in spite of
disagreements, at Yasnaya Polyana; this was a period of
peace and productivity, which gave rise to *War and Peace*
(1864–1869) and *Anna Karenina* (1873–1877).

Tolstoy had thought of writing a novel on the Decembrists, but in order to explain their period he had to study
the Napoleonic Wars, and there he stopped. *War and Peace*
gives at once a picture of the great historical events involv-
ing Napoleon, Alexander and Kutuzov, and the day-to-day
life of two families, the Rostovs and the Bolkonskys, which
Tolstoy had constructed in his usual manner by transposing
his own background into another milieu and by putting a
good deal of himself into the two main characters of Prince
Andrey and Pierre Bezukhov.

Tolstoy had the unparalleled gift of being able to impose his characters upon the memory by a few significant leitmotifs: the beautiful eyes of the ugly princess Maria, the white arms of Helen, the exuberant gestures of Natasha, who dances, runs and bounces about, overflowing with life. Napoleon at his toilet and the peasant who goes off to Smolensk in a cart leave equally vivid impressions.

It was easy to link the destinies of the two families; it would have been more difficult to tie these in with the destiny of Europe if Tolstoy had not valued the least event of each day as highly as a great victory. Great men believe in their own greatness: Napoleon believed that he was directing history, just as the child who holds on to the steering wheel believes that he is driving the cart; in reality, man is led by fate, and a victory is lost or won, not by the genius of the strategy but by mysterious factors that are felt by the private soldier, near as he is to nature. This debatable theory, on which Tolstoy dwelled too long, is rendered vivid by being incarnated in Napoleon, blinded by intelligence; in Kutuzov, the fat, peaceable man who awaits the fateful hour; and in Karatayev, the soldier who accepts his place in death as he has in life. Prince Andrey and Pierre, the one by action, the other by philosophical speculation, seek the truth on which they will build their lives between the two extremes, on the way that leads from Napoleon to Karatayev. Pierre, who learns in time from Karatayev, will eventually find peace in family life. Natasha has been tending naturally toward that truth, for like Pushkin's Tatiana, this little countess is by the nature of her soul very close to the people, very close to life. *War and Peace* is a hymn to life; there is no book more alive than this and in it beats the heart of Russia, heroic and peaceable, in battles and family scenes, suffering and song, in all the aspects of its countryside; it is the *Iliad* and the *Odyssey* of Russia.

In *Anna Karenina,* Tolstoy chose to depict the life of his own times, within the frame of the town and country life of his own aristocratic milieu. Here too are many personal memories, and the author himself appears as Levin. Two themes interlace: that of the unhappy marriage, and that of the happy life that has its own problems. Anna leaves her virtuous, dry and pedantic husband for the brilliant Vronsky, but although he is faithful and generous, she suffers and finally comes to suicide.

Many a reader has wondered why Tolstoy chose this denouement, and why he chose the epigraph "Vengeance is mine and I will repay," for, like Natasha, Anna was only obeying the instinct of life. Dostoievsky suggested an answer: no one has the right to construct his happiness on the suffering of others, and Anna sacrificed both husband and child; but Tolstoy offers no apparent moral, and we are simply presented with a moving study of a woman in love, from the first stirrings of her heart to the final tragedy.

The moral intent is more evident in the secondary theme of the novel, which depicts the happy love of Levin and Kitty; here can be seen how much Tolstoy had changed since writing *War and Peace.* Levin has his family life and the useful activity that Tolstoy had once proposed as the true purpose in life, and yet he suffers, asking himself the question, What is the point of life? in an anguish that would lead him to suicide if one of his peasants did not supply him with the answer: "Believe in God." We learn from Tolstoy in his *A Confession* (written in 1879 and published in 1882) that this interior conflict was his own, that during his years of apparent happiness, religious doubts and anguish for society had been secretly growing and that the truth was revealed to him by lowly people: "It is faith that keeps men alive." He had sought this faith along many roads, but the instinct of the people does not fail.

Therefore he decided to practice Orthodoxy, but he was too rational, and not mystical enough to find peace in it; he came to the conclusion that religion, which must be real because it gives life to men, must have changed since it was unable to satisfy his reason. He devoted himself to studying the Bible, he translated the Gospel leaving out anything which he thought doubtful, and reduced it to the principle "Love thy neighbor as thou lovest thyself." With implacable logic he deduced from it a whole doctrine of social theory, and made himself its prophet: he condemned as being contrary to the law of love, not only war, but all resistance to evil ("Turn the other cheek"), all human justice ("Thou shalt not judge"), all power based on violence and inequality—even the existence of the State; he condemned industry, which created "the slavery of our time," the possession of land beyond the work capacity of the owner; he condemned the so-called advances of civilization, luxury and even art insofar as they could not be understood by the people and thus constituted luxuries. What remained out of this universal destruction? The duty of each man to feed his family by working on the land; if all men were united by brother love, then the problems arising out of the institution of states, armies and tribunals would not arise.

Tolstoy reiterated these ideas in numerous small treatises that were published abroad but that circulated secretly in Russia. He was excommunicated by the Holy Synod, but continued to live in peace, untroubled by the government, at Yasnaya Polyana, where he was visited by flocks of enthusiastic pilgrims from all over the world. He made a gallant effort to lead a life in accordance with his principles, distributing his land between his children, digging his fields, sewing his own boots: but the opposition of his wife, the conflict between his love for his family and the injunctions of his conscience, all combined to make a tragedy of the end of his life.

Yet another conflict was destroying him: the artist in him was rebelling against his condemnation of art, and it sometimes persuaded the moralist in him that art was the best teacher; a work of art was then being born. In 1886 appeared *The Death of Ivan Ilyich,* the realistic picture of a barren life that is brightened at the hour of death; in 1895, on a similar theme, another story, *Master and Man;* in 1886 also the play *The Power of Darkness;* and in 1889 *The Kreutzer Sonata,* which shows how Tolstoy's unhappy meditations on marriage had led him to condemn the union of man and woman as being an obstacle to reaching the kingdom of heaven; once mankind understood the truth of this, it would perish, but it would be saved.

After this work—full of bitterness, which contains a striking study of sensual and jealous love—Tolstoy recovered his optimism in his last great novel, *Resurrection* (1899), which echoes the theme of *The Power of Darkness* in offering to the guilty the consolation of the possibility of redemption by confession and expiation; this is one of Dostoievsky's themes, but whereas for him redemption arose out of love, for Tolstoy it tended more from useful activity. Once again, he put in a good deal of himself, and even confessed one of his own sins, in the prince Nekhliudov, who thinks himself a man of honor until one day, acting as a jurist in a criminal trial, he recognizes the accused, the prostitute Maslova, a pure young girl he had once seduced and lost. Out of duty, and without love, he follows her to Siberia to try and expiate the sin; she too is regenerated through suffering, and refuses his sacrifice, and a new and useful life opens for both. The ending, where Tolstoy leads the reader through unfamiliar country and surroundings, seems tedious, but parts of the novel are equal in beauty to his earlier works.

But in the battle between artist and rationalist, the artist was beaten; in the battle between love of his family and the call of asceticism, the threads that bound Tolstoy were finally broken. On October 28, 1910, the old man, accompanied by his doctor, fled from Yasnaya Polyana in the hope of spending his last days in solitude; in the train he had a bad attack of pneumonia, and it was in the little stationmaster's house at Ostapovo, besieged without knowing it by a great crowd of family, journalists and the merely curious, that the man whom Turgenev had described as "the great writer of the Russian soil" drew his last breath.

Interest in the peasant way of life, already very lively, was reinforced by Tolstoy's teachings. But Gleb Uspensky (1840–1902), whose sensitive nature could not stand the hardship of life and who went mad, was only to be disillusioned by what he learned: the peasant is materialistic, attached like a vegetable to the earth and, moreover, condemned to degeneration by capitalism. Korolenko (1853–1921) retained his faith in humanity, in spite of his difficulties and his exile in Siberia; he knew that his pitiful

Makar (*Makar's Dream*), an idle Siberian *yakhout*, a drunkard and a thief, had the excuses of poverty and ignorance; he knew that the murderers in *The Murmuring Forest* were less guilty than the degenerate lord, and that the policeman who took the nihilists to prison was not responsible. His characters are simple, very close to the animals and plants of the Russian and Siberian countryside painted so lovingly by Korolenko in his novels and in his *Siberian Tales.* Kindness and tolerance flow from every page, the kindness that throughout his long life Korolenko ceaselessly bestowed upon the unfortunates of both the Tsarist and Soviet regimes.

Fin de Siècle Pessimism

The fine, healthy moral outlook of Korolenko and Tolstoy was an exception amid the depression of the end of the century. The atmosphere was heavy, the reactionaries were triumphant and the liberals, seeing all their efforts go to waste, withdrew sadly into their shells. The picture presented by the novelists is one of a dying society, which sees no possibility of a resurrection and accepts the fact. This climate is reflected in Garshin, who committed suicide, in 1888, at the age of thirty-two. His characters have "a sick conscience," and like those of Dostoievsky, are tortured by the problems of evil, but are afforded no answer by Christianity. Soldiers who die without knowing why, laborers forced to undertake inhuman tasks, even animals and plants, all are bound to suffer; like the madman in *The Red Flower,* the author sought to drag out from the earth the evil that haunted and defied him, but evil is stronger than man.

In Chekhov (1860–1904) we are given a complete picture of Russian society on the threshold of the Revolution, scattered through a great number of short stories and some plays (he wrote no long novels). His humorous short stories, written mostly in his youth, are exceptions: they are full of wit and surprises, but not without a basis of melancholy, and the over-all impression is one of tremendous sadness. Anton Chekhov was the son of a grocer in Taganrog; he studied medicine in Moscow, and even then was writing short tales to augment his income and help his family; these were soon successful, and he was able to give up his idea of a practice, and fulfill his dream of a country property. Unfortunately, he was shortly obliged to leave it and go to live in the Crimea because of his tuberculosis; although he was already very ill, he married an actress, Olga Knipper, but died soon after on holiday in the Black Forest.

He applied his acute sense of observation to the very varied circles in which he moved in both city and province; a lucid objectivity earned him the reputation of being cold, though it suffices to read his stories of childhood to feel the sensitivity this hides; it is because he did not have the faculty of some to delude himself as to the virtues of the peasants or the merits of intellectual effort. His mujiks are degraded by poverty and alcohol, their faith is merely superstition, their habits bestial; noble families vegetate on their ruined country seats, poverty-stricken and without the energy to adapt themselves to the new conditions. The impecunious life of the artisans, and the luxurious, narrow life of the rich businessmen (*Three Years*), are equally lacking in ideals. To be sure, there are many students who burn to devote themselves to a liberal task, but this flame soon dies in the country doctor, burdened with work and isolated among ignorance. The civil servant, the judge, the teacher—bound in by the mediocrity of the small town, spied upon by informants—either take fearful shelter from life (*The Man in the Box*), or, prostrate before their superiors, seek advancement and honors. Even the high-class intellectual, the artist and the scholar are prisoners of routine, and the teacher in *A Dreary Story* replies "I do not know" to the girl who asks him for a principle by which to live. The clutching degradation of everyday life, which neither love nor ideals can resist, the futility of all effort, are the themes at the basis of Chekhov's work. His characters do not struggle: they await with resignation the moment when they will have to live no longer.

The characters of the poet, novelist and playwright Fedor Sologub (1863–1926), on the contrary, are not resigned: they hate life; all of them, even the children, are haunted by a death wish (*Death through a Diary, The Fiancée in Mourning*). Those who think they are alive are already ghosts, even more so than the rest. His striking novel *The Little Demon* radiates the fetid atmosphere of a small town, with its boredom, its vodka, its petty arguments, anonymous letters and denunciations; the abject Peredonov is the epitome of all this.

Gorky

It is easy to imagine the sense of relief with which the public, in the midst of all this depression, suddenly heard the insolent laughter of Gorky's vagabonds! They were not tired of life, in spite of all its misery and danger; they attacked it with gusto, unimpeded by scruples. Maxim Gorky, born Alexis Peshkov in 1868, was brought up at Nizhni-Novgorod in a rough artisan family; from the age of ten he tried all kinds of work, and wandered from one town to another—as a dock hand in Odessa, a baker in Kazan, a railway worker in Tiflis. He had read at random, and particularly French writers—Balzac, the elder Dumas, Ponson du Terrail. In 1892 he published his first short story, *Makar Chudra,* in the paper *The Caucasus;* then he received the patronage of Korolenko, and success came with amazing speed, abroad as well as in Russia. Soon his plays (*The Lower Depths,* 1902) added to his celebrity.

The first short stories of Gorky are extremely romantic —neither the landscapes nor the characters give the impression of being quite real, but this very romanticism brought a breath of fresh air to a public satiated with psychological subtleties. Beneath the brilliant sunlight and the great wind of the southern steppes his sweeping strokes depict the adventurers, smugglers and dock hands, who are afraid of nothing—hard work, debauchery or crime—and who have only contempt for the ordered life of the city-dweller and the peasant. Here was a new force, a new strength, even in those who had sunk to the lowest level.

But a change was taking place in Gorky, a change that led him from anarchism to Marxism and from romanticism to realism. The vagabonds give way to artisans and tradesmen, such as he had known as a child, in *Foma Gordeyev, Matvey Kozhemyakin* and much later (1925) *The Artamonov Affair,* the story of the rise and fall of a bourgeois family; these are somber pictures indeed. But Gorky balanced these mean upper- and lower-middle classes with the workmen who were preparing the Revolution, and who through discipline had retained the ardor of his earlier heroes. The pervading political tone sometimes mars the verisimilitude of the characters in *Mother*, although there are some fine passages; Gorky's last novel, *The Life of Klim Samgin*, shows the Revolution in full swing.

But nowhere is his evocative power so great as when he writes of his own youth. Not one of his imaginary characters is as alive as the terrifying grandfather, the drunken and bestial uncles, the sweet-natured and resigned grandmother in *Childhood*, nor as the author himself, sensitive and already rebelling, as we see him in this first volume of memories and in those that followed. It was in this way that he was able to return in thought to his native land; for after the failure of the Revolution in 1905, he had to leave Russia and, after spending some time in New York, he settled in Capri. He returned to Russia twice, the first time during the war, when he was able to witness the triumph of the Revolution and to champion intellectual values, and the second time, in 1936, to die there.

Realists and Symbolists

Of the same political opinions as Gorky, but of quite a different temperament, was Leonid Andreyev (1871–1921), a novelist and playwright. He was less interested in the external world than in the mystery of fate; he tended to give symbolic values to his characters, and death pervades his work as it does that of Sologub. *The Seven That Were*

Hanged examines the reactions of seven condemned men, while *The Yoke of War* studies the effects of the great events on an ordinary soldier of the rear guard.

Kuprin, a follower of Gorky, renders very powerfully the depressing atmosphere of a small garrison town (*The Duel*), the excitement of a great port (*Gambrinus*), the life of prostitutes (*The Ditch*); but his forays into reasoning interrupt the action too often. The Nobel Prize-winner, Ivan Bunin (1870–1953), should not be reproached with being coldly objective, whether his incisive talent, his precise and colorful style, are used to depict peasants in a dreary country setting (*The Village*), or to describe the return journey made by *The Gentleman from San Francisco*, who sets out full of life and full of projects, and returns in his coffin.

Side by side with the realistic novel, there emerged at the very end of the nineteenth century a contrasting trend akin to the rise of symbolist poetry. For Merezhkovsky, the historical novel is only a means of expressing the ideas that fill his works (poetry, drama and criticism): he seeks a reconciliation between Christianity and paganism, between the Greek spirit and the Nazarean spirit, and the three phases of this struggle are represented by *Julian the Apostate, Leonardo da Vinci* and *Peter and Alexis,* in the trilogy *Christ and Antichrist.*

The poet Andrei Bely is concerned with the eternal problem of Russia's relations with the East or the West. *The Silver Dove* (1910) tells of the tragic end that befalls a young intellectual who is swallowed up by a sect of sensual and fanatical mystics. *Petersburg* is for Bely an unreal city, the fruit of Peter the First's imagination, but even the people of *Moscow* are only vague phantoms; everything is illusion to the dreamy and sensitive poet who is revealed to us in the autobiographical novel of his childhood, *Kotik Letayev,* and in his *The Memoirs of an Eccentric.*

Alexis Remizov, a great admirer of Gogol and Dostoievsky, did not hesitate in his choice: confronted with the sad burden of contemporary life evoked in his *The Sisters of the Cross* and *The Fifth Pestilence,* he sought refuge in the old traditions of Russia, in the fairy tales and legends that he retells in a new and subtle symbolic form.

Abundant and varied though it still was on the eve of the Revolution, the golden age of the novelistic tradition had passed. The Revolution brought it new themes.

7 / The Theatre in the Nineteenth Century

In Russia the history of the theatre is not so brilliant as that of the novel. The Russian novel has had a remarkable influence on the Western novel; the Russian theatre has produced some masterpieces, but it has not originated any new forms—unless one includes methods of scenic realization.

Historical Plays

After romanticism, drama with Russian history as a theme never lost its prestige in the eyes of a public that had applauded Mey's *Pskovitianka* and *The Tsar's Betrothed*, the plays of Kukolnik, and above all, Count Alexis

Tolstoy's trilogy *The Death of Ivan the Terrible, Tsar Fedor Ioannovich* and *Tsar Boris* (1867–1870). Tolstoy's tragedies followed Schiller's in form; they were influenced considerably not only by the latter, but also by Shakespeare and by Pushkin. They are well worthy of comparison with their models in their vivid re-creation of the past, their delineation of character, and the beauty of their verse. Although they cannot be compared with *Boris Godunov,* and although Tolstoy had not the brilliant inspiration of Pushkin, he did have a much better sense of theatre. His *Boris* is in no way a replica; hardly troubled at all by remorse, motivated both by his own ambition and by the national cause, he is completely devoted to action. The characters of the other two tsars are even more skillfully analyzed: there is the striking figure of Ivan the Terrible, on the verge of death itself, hesitating between remorse and pride, between a fear of hell and a love of debauchery, a monarch so accustomed to identify himself with his empire that he forced it to take part even in the waverings of his soul, and humiliated it in humiliating himself. As a contrast, his son, Fedor, good, weak and pious, reminds one of some of Dostoievsky's most innocent characters. Tolstoy has a gift for choosing incidents that appeal to the imagination, for his balance of scenes, for leaving the audience at the end of the act with a strong impression, emphasized by a well-turned line. Provided as they were with splendidly luxurious costumes and décor, these tragedies were among the most brilliant spectacles of the Moscow Art Theatre.

The Theatre of Manners

Nevertheless it was in the comedy of manners that Russian talent most excelled itself. Fonvizin in the eighteenth century and Griboyedov in the romantic age were followed quite naturally in this path by Gogol. He made his debut with some short comic pieces: *The Vladimir Order, Marriage,* amusing studies of the "merchant" society and of a bridegroom who could not make up his mind, and then *Revizor* (1836), in which he attained to mastership. The idea came to him from a true story told him by Pushkin: a young man passing through a small village is suspected by the local officials, who have uneasy consciences, of being an inspector sent, incognito, to investigate their behavior; he is entertained, heaped with favors, and the truth is not revealed until after his departure. The comedy of misunderstandings and of characters that are almost caricatures does not really hide the somber colors of the whole picture: these officials, from the governor down, are all without any principles and accept gratuities according to rank—often taking more than their rank merits; in contrast, the unwitting imposter, boastful and unscrupulous as he is, seems on the whole a less unsympathetic character. The play had considerable success, to a degree that startled the author, who maintained that he had set out merely with the intention of making the audience laugh.

Alexander Ostrovsky (1833–1886), of all the Russian writers, was almost the only one to devote all his energies to the theatre. He left some historical plays, in imitation of

Shakespeare's, and a charming narrative play called *Sne-gurochka*. But the most important part of his work is a collection of about fifty comedies of manners. A playwright in every sense of the word, he knew how to be detached, and refused to set out any theory; his morality is very simple and centered on honesty and common sense. His plots are likewise simple: he studies character and customs. He introduced many Russians to the world of the Moscow "merchants," a world separate from the rest, in which he himself had grown up; in its old quarter of the town, on the south bank of the river Moskva, it had retained its own laws and its own language, and unlike the Europeanized aristocracy had continued to live as it had in the time of the *Domostroi*. Now the "merchant," devoted as he was to money, combined the unscrupulousness of an oriental trader with modern trickery, sometimes going as far as pretended bankruptcy (*The Bankrupt, or Among Friends One Can Always Come to Terms*). He accumulated riches, not avariciously, but for ostentatious effect: *Poverty Is Not a Vice,* insists an extraordinary Jourdain, more clownish even than Molière's character, bursting with self-satisfied pride because he has cut his beard and is drinking champagne. The merchant despises all merit that has no commercial value; he is completely indifferent to intellectual activity, he makes no effort to teach his children and retains all the old superstitions. He reigns as a dreaded tyrant over family and employees. His wife, a slave adorned with jewels, married according to her father's wishes and merely changed masters; she rarely rebels.

Nevertheless there is the passionate and mystical Catherine in *The Storm:* suffocating between a tyrannical mother-in-law and a feeble husband, she allows herself to be seduced by her lover, but, goaded by remorse, she confesses her sin and kills herself. For woman in this society imagines no other existence than that imposed upon her by tradition, no amusement in her seclusion other than the religious offices to be attended and the songs sung by the servants. If she marries out of her station she is equally unhappy (*Don't Put Yourself in Another's Sledge*).

Ostrovsky had no more indulgence for the other social classes. *The Ward, The Forest, The Sheep and the Wolves,* take us into the country seats of the gentry, which are ruled over by tyrannical and bigoted old women who hide stormy pasts, ancient love affairs or base cupidity beneath their hypocrisy. Officeholders are also the slaves of money. The author's sympathies seem to be with the people of the theatre, whose absurdity he reveals as well as their disinterestedness (*The Forest*), and with the individualists, such as Liubim Tortsov in *Poverty Is Not a Vice*, who has a generous heart in the midst of his downfall. In spite of this, his plays rarely leave a bitter taste in the mouth; many seem to brighten up with the denouement and are carefully poised between the sad and the comic; the language is spicy and rich in popular turns of phrase. The best among them are still staged today.

Another play, which since 1855 has never ceased to be put on, is *The Wedding of Krechinsky,* by Sukhovo-Kobylin. It owes its continuing popularity to its neat plot and clever dialogue.

As with the novel, the theatre took an interest in peasant manners and ways of life. *The Judgment of Men Is Not the Judgment of God,* by Potekhin (1854), and *A Bitter*

Fate, by Pisemsky (1858), in this genre were the forerunners of *Power of Darkness,* by Leo Tolstoy. This was written in 1886, and produced in Russia in 1895 only after a production in Paris in 1888 at the Théâtre Antoine; it is undoubtedly the greatest work in Russian drama. It presents a picture of peasant life that, without ever becoming merely documentary, tells us about the customs, festivals and language of a village in the Tula region; but it is above all a psychological study that reaches beyond its setting and period. Tolstoy follows step by step the inexorable invasion of evil in a mind that has been led by weakness to commit one crime and sinks further and further into the mire, until at last it is freed by confession and expiation. The characters are both realistic and symbolic: Old Matrena, the hypocritical and grasping peasant, who, with a prayer always ready on her lips, yet plotting crime after crime, represents the power of evil, whereas the simple and almost ridiculous Akim is the embodiment of good. They wrestle over the soul of their son just as good and evil wrestle in every human soul. Tolstoy's religious ideas are never expressed in abstract form, and the tragic intensity of the action—which becomes almost unbearably realistic in the infanticide scene—is never broken.

Unfortunately, there is not the same objectivity in *And Light Shines in the Darkness,* a long play that is interesting largely because of its autobiographical value. *The Living Corpse* also reveals, although more discreetly, Tolstoy's suffering and his need to escape. One more characteristic should also be noted, a rather unexpected one: Tolstoy is the author of an amusing anti-spiritualist comedy, *The*

Fruits of Enlightenment, which proves, if any proof is needed, the variety of his gifts as a writer.

It is to be regretted that Turgenev renounced the theatre so early on: his juvenilia created atmosphere skillfully and are reminiscent of Chekhov. This is particularly true of *A Month in the Country,* which has almost no plot but is a fine psychological study.

Even more than his novels, Chekhov's plays make a strong contrast to Russian drama as a whole. The latter delights in turning comedy into caricature, and suffering into agony; it loves to argue a theory (this had to be done more carefully in the theatre, which was so closely censored). Chekhov's plays, on the other hand, are in half-tones, and suggest more than they actually show. They are not void of plot, nor even of tragic element, but the most important things go on in people's thoughts, in souls that are shy of revealing themselves. The dialogue is carefully restrained, with few passionate outbursts, and almost no discussion of ideas; but the evocative power is intense. *The Sea Gull* (1896) involves the milieu of writers and actors; *The Three Sisters* (1902), a small, sleepy town; *Uncle Vanya* (1900) and *The Cherry Orchard* (1904) are about the decay of the country nobility. Each hints of a vague boredom and lassitude: there is an atmosphere of stagnant water and dead leaves, as in many of the novels; Chekhov's heroes lack the courage to react. The three sisters will never leave for Moscow, Uncle Vanya and his niece will go on sadly making up the accounts of the property until the very day when the first cherry trees fall under the axe of the man who has bought it. It is a dying world.

Chekhov's example had a lot to do with the early interest that Gorky had in the theatre: he, too, depicted the narrowness of the small town (*The Craftsmen*) and the world of the artists (*The Holiday-Makers*); and *Children of the Sun* criticizes the milieu of the "cultured," recalling *A Dreamy Story*. But Gorky was by temperament as passionate, extravagant and anxious to express his beliefs as Chekhov was reserved. Much of the young Gorky's romanticism remains in his masterpiece *The Lower Depths* (1902); in this, from a sordid night-refuge for gallow-birds, there comes a cry of faith in the future of humanity. The later plays of Gorky, written before and after the Revolution, became more and more concerned with politics.

Leonid Andreyev wrote very many different works for the theatre, all colored with the same pessimism that can be felt in his novels. *Savva* (1906) rebels against destiny, seeks to deprive men of their faith, in order that they will be confronted plainly with their own misery "naked, upon the naked earth." His allegorical plays, and in particular *The Life of Man*, are essays in philosophy, lacking in any real depth.

Blok's fine symbolic plays (*The Knight, The Rose and the Cross, The Minstrel, The King in the Marketplace*) should be read: they belong more to poetry than to the stage. The same applies to the noble tragedies of Vyacheslav Ivanov, *Tantalus* and *Prometheus*, which borrowed both structure and subject matter from Greece.

Even the most rapid survey of the history of Russian drama should not pass over the excellent interpretations made by actors and producers, and in particular, the role of the Moscow Art Theatre, founded in 1898 by Stanislavsky (the assumed name of an industrialist, K. Alexeyev) and Nemirovich-Danchenko. This theatre has repeatedly given quite unforgettable performances of Alexis Tolstoy's tragedies, of *Power of Darkness, The Lower Depths,* of the plays of Chekhov and of many others, all remarkable for the complete devotion shown to the work, for the unity among the actors of the companies, and for the scrupulously realistic décor, authentic down to the smallest detail. However, there was a reaction to this complete realism: at the beginning of the twentieth century another tendency appeared, which simplified décor and allowed a free rein to the imagination. In this respect Meyerhold and Vakhtangov were names known all over Europe.

8 / *Post-Romantic Poetry*

From 1840 on, Russian literature was a battlefield, and poetry a weapon. A few poets, however, who were the disciples of Pushkin, refused to "take up a broom and sweep the streets," and so there were two opposing ideas. Some considered that the poet was above all else a citizen, and some considered that he was above all else an artist. It is not surprising to find that the former were liberals, living among the people, and that the poets who advocated art for art's sake were conservative aristocrats. The liberals may have found life harder, but glory was after all theirs, while their opponents were slighted and slandered.

Poetry as a Weapon

Nikolay Nekrasov (1821–1877) was the greatest of
these writers. When Dostoievsky, who did not share his
ideas, but admired his talent, was speaking at his grave, he
placed him equal to Pushkin and Lermontov; the crowd
enthusiastically shouted: "Even greater!" Born into the lower
ranks of the nobility, he had been brought up in the country, where his father's harshness and the misery of the
peasants had made a deep impression on him. Resolving
not to become an officer in the army, he eked out a living
until his friendship with Belinsky smoothed his career as
a journalist. He directed *The Contemporary,* and later
Annals of the Fatherland, to both of which he welcomed
young talent. He called his own inspiration "the muse of
vengeance and mourning"; "I have been chosen, my people,
to sing of your suffering," he used to say. His verse leaves
little room for his own emotions, except pity for this unfortunate people. He depicts the misery of the towns, of
the small, impecunious official, of the laborer who toils to
build a railroad that he will never use; he also depicts the
misery of the country, of the peasant, and of the peasant's
wife, who works in the fields and in the cottage, and who,
in the forest where she has gone to gather wood, falls
asleep in the snow never to awake again (*Frost the Red-
nosed*). *Who Is Happy in Russia?* is the agonized question
in the title of Nekrasov's longest poem. It was never finished,
but the reader well knows that the seven peasants who
make a vow to find a happy man will seek in vain. The

structure of Nekrasov's poems is rough and prosaic at times, but it often moves with grandeur and passion.

Nadson was to follow in his footsteps, but he died in 1887, at the age of twenty-five. Affected with tuberculosis, and feeling himself a condemned man, he had a desperate desire to live and to love, which struggled within him with his decision to devote himself to the cause of the lower classes. This inner conflict often gives a touch of poignancy to a rather unpolished piece of work. This people so pitied by Nekrasov and Nadson itself produced Nikitin (1824–1861); he has been called a second Koltsov because his poems are of a popular nature, and because of his charming descriptions, but his bitter feeling for the misery of the peasants is quite different from Koltsov's.

The Slavophiles also often made use of poetry to defend their beliefs, but the powerful verses of Khomyakov take second place in his work. However, a poet such as Tyutchev, who could, when occasion demanded, express political opinions, was more at home in the field of pure art.

"Pure" Poetry

Tyutchev (1803–1873) was of Pushkin's generation, although his first collection of poems did not appear until 1854. He was a diplomat and lived for a long time in Germany, and his philosophy was founded on Schelling and Schopenhauer; he aspired to the serenity of Goethe and sympathized with the pessimism of Heine. He wrote some remarkably good translations in verse from various German poets. A long love affair, which violently upset his life after he had reached middle age, was to enrich his poetry. He had a hidden shyness, nevertheless, and the agonizing feeling of the powerlessness of words. Mystery is everywhere, in the human soul and in nature; the poet accepts this world, of which he is a part, but, far from conceiving it as being in perfect harmony, he is terrified of the dormant chaos, of the abysses beneath his feet and the chasms of his own mind, of the stirring of a subconscious only weakly controlled by reason. This solemn poetry, so rich in thought and so studied in form, had to await the coming of symbolism, which it heralded, to be appreciated. Even then it could be fully appreciated only by the elect.

Alexis Tolstoy (1817–1875) alone of the poets of "pure" art was able to move a great number of readers. Moreover, he never allowed himself to follow any poetic fashion; he was only moved to attack by tendentious poetry, and this in the name of the beauty to which he was so passionately devoted, sensitive, unfaltering and optimistically courageous as he was. He would have liked to have devoted himself entirely to this cult of beauty, but was prevented from doing so by his post as aide-de-camp to Alexander II, whose childhood friend he had been. He was released from this only in 1861, but from that time on, living sometimes in the West and sometimes in Russia, he gave himself up to poetry and to the great love that animated his life. His work includes the dramatic trilogy that has been studied earlier in this book, a historical novel in the manner of Walter Scott also set in the time of Ivan the Terrible, *Prince Serebryany,* and much lyrical poetry. He was a pantheist, like Tyutchev, but more confident and optimistic: "The murmur of the waters, the breath of the flowers, all seem to me a promise of another, far-off beauty." Love and art enabled the soul to commune with this eternal beauty. This idealism did not prevent Tolstoy from being aware of the outside world, and of the characteristics of the countryside where he lived, nor from keeping up his mocking, cheerful good sense (when young he and his cousins had composed the witty aphorisms of *Kozma Prutkov*). His popular heroic poems about ancient Russia are a chronicle of the times, painted in the most brilliant of colors.

Fet (1820–1892) was a purely lyrical poet, and his work is perhaps the most lyrical of all Russian poetry by virtue of its musical form, in which the sounds suggest more than the mere meaning of the words. Nevertheless he was a practical and realistic man, the son of a German (his father's name, Shenshin, he was able to use only late in life). He was the owner of a model farm, and very proud of the results of his cultivation; he published some verse in his youth, but it was not until very much later that he returned to poetry, and together with some translations of Goethe, Heine and Hafiz, published his finest collection, *Fires of Evening*. His concept of nature recalls both Tyutchev and Tolstoy: he is aware of mystery and trembles at it, but he turns from the abyss to rejoice in the charm of hours during which a secret communion melts his heart with the stirrings of spring, the languor of the undergrowth in summer, the sparkle of a starry night. A few rippling, crystalline lines are enough for him to conjure up this special magic.

Apollo Maykov (1821–1897) was much attracted by antiquity and wrote, as well as a play set in the period of Nero, some pleasant poems in the manner of Anacreon, and some translations. Polonsky (1820–1898) showed some signs of liberal tendencies, but is at his best when in reminiscent or contemplative poetry. The Grand Duke Konstantin Konstantinovich, who signed his work K. R., is simple and charming. Apukhtin is often hampered by banalities. Sluchevsky sometimes shows a sudden streak of fantasy that links him with the symbolists. However, these are all second-rate poets.

Symbolism

There was no poetic revival until early in 1900. Born in the West, symbolism spread across Europe just as romanticism had done a century earlier. The voices of Baudelaire, Verlaine, Poe, Wilde, Hauptmann and Stefan George rang out in rebellion against the reigning prose and utilitarian materialism. In Russia, where realism and a spirit of conflict had invaded poetry to a greater extent than elsewhere, this revolt met with less understanding. The poets of the new school were quickly branded reactionaries; but the welcome given by the greatest among them to the Revolution was proof enough that these individualists were more revolutionary in spirit than the literary conformists.

In 1895 a collection called *Russian Symbolists* appeared; as well as translations of Verlaine, Poe and Maeterlinck, it included poems by Bryusov and others unknown to the public, and was followed by two others. The same year saw the appearance of a volume of poems that Bryusov boldly called *Masterpieces,* and Balmont's *Boundless Space,* which had been preceded in 1894 by *Under the Northern Sky.* In the following years, Bryusov, Balmont, Merezhkovsky, Zinaida Hippius and Sologub struggled to convince an indignant or jeering public of the new point of view. Their names appeared together again in the poetical almanac, *Flowers of the North,* and then in the periodical *The Scales.* Although these poets were lumped together under the name of "decadents," and were united in supporting the rights of art against the "tendencies," they were very different from each other in temperament.

Some were adamant against the careless form into which so many of their predecessors had slipped, and like consummate artists fashioned intricate and perfect verses. They used new meters, more supple rhymes and assonances, and they sought out original images. The most brilliant among them was Balmont, perhaps too brilliant: he was endowed with a dazzling virtuosity that left little room for emotion, but that glinted and sparkled with all the lights and music of a nature in which the poet became lost in delight. Valery Bryusov did not have this faculty, and his poetry sometimes gives the impression of deliberately looking for difficulties to overcome, but he often possesses a firmness and breadth that could almost be called classic.

Other poets escaped prosaic reality by their thought rather than by form. They attempted to express the inexpressible, the unknown that surrounds the superficial appearance of life. In his poetry and in his short stories Sologub reveals his longing for death. The same can be said of Annensky, who translated his favorite, Verlaine, and, like Tyutchev, felt the agony of chaos lying like a menace beneath the ordered surface of things. On the other hand, the philosopher Vladimir Soloviev sounded a note of hope, sang the call of the beyond, the mediation of the Eternal

Feminine, and union with God. His ideas inspired the Petersburg poets who met in the salon of Merezhkovsky and his wife Zinaida Hippius, or in the "tower" of Vyacheslav Ivanov. Andrey Bely (his real name was Bugayev) avowed himself a disciple of Soloviev, but in his search for truth his soul is more tormented, falling from exultation (*Gold in Azure*) to discouragement (*Ashes*); nevertheless in the darkest hours he kept his faith in Russia, in the value of redemption through her suffering: when the Revolution came he cried out in fervor: "Christ is risen again!" He approaches Alexander Blok in his thinking, but without attaining the latter's evocative power and supreme simplicity.

Blok (1880–1921) was a very great poet: a dreamer and a solitary, he has remained in the memory of all those who knew his work, however slightly, as almost the very incarnation of poetry. He was born of a family of great intellectuals, very cultivated and westernized himself, and at the beginning of his career he seemed very far from the people in whose cause he so magnificently raised his voice in their most tragic hour. His first poems (*Verses for the Beautiful Lady*) celebrated, as Soloviev had done, the mysterious Initiatrice whose mission is to lead man toward Truth. She is not of this earth, although she can, once upon earth, incarnate herself for the chosen in a great love; she can be the Muse, the Virgin or the Evening Star; she can be felt in the breath of spring, in the whiteness of the moonlight. But slowly an agonizing fear fills the poet's soul: supposing She does not exist, or worse still, is merely a common prostitute? Now it is not in a décor misty with dreams, but in a suburban cabaret that the *Unknown* appears to him, and there he tries to define the enigma in her eyes behind the dark veil. There followed a long period of confusion during which sudden upsurges of *joie de vivre (Poems of Italy)* were quickly stifled by the sad banality of the days, and Blok tried to drown his sorrows in debauchery and alcohol. However, like Bely he became more and more absorbed in the cult of Russia, which replaced the Beautiful Lady of earlier times in his heart. He loved Russia, both in the glory of her past (*Kulikovo*) and in the sorrows of her present. And so it was that when the Revolution came, this solitary intellectual spontaneously joined the cause of his people. In the *Scythians* he gave a solemn warning to the Western powers who intervened at the time; *The Twelve* (winter 1918) is the greatest poem the Revolution inspired; it is a strange poem, mingling all kinds of rhythms and tones, mixing scenes of growing realism with grandiose flights of fancy; the howling winter wind and the gusts of snow carry with them the breath of the Revolution, guided by Christ crowned with roses, who precedes the twelve Red soldiers. In this way Blok the poet wholeheartedly joined with the enthusiasm of the people; but the man himself was physically ill-equipped to face the hard conditions of those terrible years: he died a sad death in 1921.

Acmeists and Futurists

The genius of Blok overflowed the bounds of symbolism just as that of Pushkin overflowed all definitions of romanticism. Symbolism declined even as it evolved, and already other trends were confronting it. On one side there were Kuzmin and the "Acmeists," with Gumilev, Anna

Akhmatova, Osip Mandelstamm and Sergey Gorodetsky; to the symbolist's obsession with death they opposed a healthy love of life, to their abstractions and symbols a clarity, and to their music a firm and precise pattern. In the case of Khodasevich, symbolist influences are combined with a measured and cruel precision. This group of poets, with slight variations, was moving toward a new classicism.

On the other side, almost at the same time, the Futurists appeared. They were greeted with the same derision as the symbolists had been in 1895. They were violently opposed to the latter; they declared, at least in their childish desire to create a scandal at their debut, that they would sweep away the past and reject the logic of thought. They would take as their starting point the word *qua* word, because "the word is greater than the meaning." We will meet this school of poetry, and in particular Vladimir Mayakovsky, with the Revolution.

9 / After the Revolution*

Poetry

When the Revolution overturned the whole edifice of Tsarist Russia, so long undermined anyway, there was reason
to fear that literature might be buried beneath the ruins.
With some exceptions (Blok, Bely, Bryusov, Gorky) most
well-known writers either emigrated or stopped writing.
But although prose remained silent until about 1920, poetry
was intensely active during the first months of the Revolution. Poetry is, of course, more capable at any time of
meeting the challenge of great events; moreover, in this

* This chapter has been written with the kind help of Mme.
Jeanne Rude.

field the literary Revolution had preceded the social Revolution, and the latter found many true poets ready to sing its praises. We have noted that the finest poetry that it inspired was Blok's *The Twelve;* and the art of Yesenin and Mayakovsky was formed before the Revolution. The Revolution brought on a fever of inspiration, a poetic intoxication that we cannot but admire when we think of the conditions in which the poets were writing—scribbling their poems on a wall or a table for want of paper, and later printing them on coarse packing paper, declaiming them in the cafés and the streets. The public, although ravaged by civil war and famine, jostled to hear them, and fiercely took sides.

There were opposing schools: Futurists, including Severyanin, Khlebnikov, Mayakovsky, Aseyev and Burlyuk; Imaginists, like Yesenin, Marienhof, Cherchenyevich and Kusikov; and Impressionists, Expressionists, Constructivists, Functionists, Nitchevoyists and so on. They had in common the desire to give the new world a new poetry; but in order to do this, they rather too often used studied forms, images and neologisms that make their work difficult to understand. Theirs was a refined and aristocratic art, very far removed from the people. The best among them quickly turned from the excesses against which Lunacharsky so rightly protested.

Special mention should be made of three peasant-poets of the same stock as Koltsov: Klytchkov, Klyuyev and Yesenin. They remained basically traditionalist, expecting that the Revolution, messiah-like, would reveal the true face of peasant Russia; they abhorred industrial progress. Klytchkov was fundamentally a graphic writer, Klyuyev a mystic and Sergey Yesenin (1895–1925) was above all an incomparable landscape artist. All his work is full of nostalgia for the village near Ryazan where he spent his childhood, without, however, having any experience of the hard work that went on in the fields. From a distance of time he envelops it in the rosy light of memory and the atmosphere of holy legend. He uses brand-new images, inspired by rural life and domestic animals; he abused these during his "imaginist" period, but his best poetry is simple and musical. He was destroyed by city life and success, and above all by his marriage to Isadora Duncan; he followed her to France and America, feeling himself a foreigner in foreign countries, and still a foreigner on his return to his own country. He felt cheated by a Revolution very different from the one he had envisaged and sung, by a Revolution that saw the triumph of the machine; he took refuge in alcohol (*Moscow of the Cabarets, Confession of a Hooligan*), and then in death: "My poetry is no longer necessary here, and doubtless I am myself no longer necessary."

Vladimir Mayakovsky (born in 1892, he also committed suicide in 1934) was quite different in temperament: he was vigorous and fundamentally a revolutionary. This giant from the Caucasus, strong and ardent, was only attracted to Futurism in a spirit of revolt against the bourgeois literary traditions. His violent, impetuously romantic lyricism has nothing in common with Yesenin's. In his first poems he sang magnificently of love (*The Flute of Vertebrae*), but the Revolution transformed his talents: all "self" vanished before the will to serve; he vowed "all his resounding strength as a poet" to the "class that is attacking," and brandished his verse "as a Party ticket"; he did not disdain to make himself the "advocate of boiled water," for sickness is also an enemy; he knew how to convey with grandeur the agony of a people in his poem on the death of Lenin, the hope of a people in 150,000,000, a virulent attack on capitalist society. His technique is revolutionary also, his syntax is ragged, his vocabulary deliberately vulgar and his imagery and rhythms unexpected. His sonorous lines, emphatically rhythmical, are made to be spoken aloud; the powerful voice of the poet engraved them upon the hearts of the crowds. The ardor of his political convictions did not dampen the humor that sparkles in the comedy *The Bedbug*, and that mingles with the grandiose in *Mystery-Bouffe*, bringing forward the universal triumph of the proletariat.

Bezymiensky, Jarov, Utkin and Golodny were far less talented, but they with other proletarian poets also put themselves at the service of Communism. Bezymiensky's verse is full of the optimism that was intended to be the inspiration of the young people. Demian Biedny, whose fables and quatrains became very popular, wrote verse that is hardly more than rhyming prose.

However, true lyrical poetry survived in the work of proletarian poets like Svetlov and Kazin, but above all with a group of poets who carried on in the earlier tradition: Mandelstamm, Anna Akhmatova and Boris Pasternak (1890–1960), who dared to affirm the complete freedom of art. "The only task for art is to be brilliantly achieved," he said; ". . . for me, art has never seemed to be an object or an aspect of form, but rather a mysterious and hidden element of the contents." The title of a collection of work published in 1922, *My Sister Life*, would suit all his works. He was just as aware of the smallest and simplest aspects of the world of the senses as he was of the largest, and transfigured them all in his dream. In proclaiming his cult of life, he has at times a vital impulse and pantheistic tendencies that remind one of Tyutchev, and at other times he rediscovers the simplicity of Russian faith, to sing of the Christmas Star. His style, difficult in his early poems and with unusually disjointed metaphors, gradually evolved toward great simplicity. (The same can be said of his prose, from *Safe-Conduct* to *Doctor Zhivago*.) His poetry is almost classic in rhythm.

Novels of the Civil War

By about 1920 prose had raised its head again and the novel had supplanted poetry in depicting reality and serving the new State. The first Soviet novelists were less independent of their forerunners than they themselves believed in the intoxication of their debut. But their art did have new characteristics: they were fond of scenes presented in a quick succession recalling cinema technique, intense action, numerous characters and rather scanty psychological characterization. Chekhov's despondent intellectuals, prone to gloomy self-analysis, gave place to partisans and soldiers who were passionate and savage, with no respect for human life, either their own or their neighbors'. The language was also quick, with short sentences and a tendency toward such dialogue with popular and deliberately chosen dialectical expressions. It was a form suited to subjects inspired only by the Revolution and the Civil War. The earliest of these novels are striking in a kind of ferocious romanticism, a mixture of exultation and cruel irony, and an impetuous and savage eagerness. Then as time mellowed the events the tone became calmer and the outlook widened, dialogue gave place to narrative, and psychology deepened.

Babel, who had made an unsuccessful attempt in literature before the war and then had served in Budenny's division, described some episodes of the war in *Red Cavalry*. This is a collection of stories reminiscent of Tolstoy in technique but quite different in their ardor and irony. He emphasizes the cruelty of life and loves its tragic beauty; his scenes of killings, pillages and rape, all of an extreme crudity, are shot through with a dry precision and a kind of lyricism. His *Jewish Stories* (he was himself a Jew and from Odessa) describe the thieves of Odessa in the same cruelly picturesque way.

Romanticism also colors the work of the Siberian Vsevolod Ivanov; he had an adventurous life that made him in turn printer, sailor, fakir and soldier, and he wrote tales in which the Revolution surges on like a storm across the steppes of Asia. For his partisans (*Partisans, Armored Train No. 14-69*), for his peasants in revolt (*Blue Sands*) living in the heart of a savage nature and in constant danger, life takes on all its primitive power: hunger, cold, scorching heat, anger, love and hatred. "You can always make another man, given one man"; "Nothing is easier than killing a man"; "We are animals and animals need blood."

The woman novelist Seyfulina, a governess of Tartar origin, also describes Siberia. With her peasants emancipated by the Revolution (*Virineya*) and her bands of wandering children (*Outlaws*), her deliberately coarse realism had none of the color of Ivanov's.

Pilnyak, the author of *The Naked Year*, was on the

contrary an extremely cultured writer, who had the peculi-
arity of being a traditional revolutionary and a Slavophile.
He saw in the Revolution a return to the Russia that had
antedated Peter I, to a national spirit freed from Western
influence. He was attached to the "izbas, unchanged for a
thousand years," and to "the wisdom of the people, the ancient wisdom of our country"; he saw the Bolsheviks as
"leather jackets with no traces of sentiment" and as de-
scendants of the *bogatyrs:* like one of his own characters,
he opposed them deliberately to the Communists, who were
full of foreign ideas.

Among the most popular novels of the early part of the
Revolution must be mentioned Furmanov's *Tchapaev,* and
in particular, Nicolas Ostrovsky's *And the Steel Was
Tempered,* an autobiographical novel, the story of the form-
ing of a character. A young militant Communist, a soldier,
sick and almost blind, wants to go on serving his country:
he is presented as an example of Soviet youth.

Just as the works devoted to the Revolution improved
with the passage of time, so they became better constructed
and psychology played a greater part in them. Fadeyev's
Rout (1927), like the stories of Ivanov, depicted the war in
Asia, but with less primitive strength and a more delicate
study of character. The return to literary tradition was even
more marked in Sholokhov's *And Quiet Flows the Don,*
which was begun in 1930; it borrows from *War and Peace*
a mingling of war scenes and family scenes, of historical
and imaginary characters. Already there is a hint of imparti-
ality, which does justice to the courage and sincerity of the
White Russians. The author, born among the Cossacks of
the Don and speaking their language, excels in colorful

descriptions of the way of life of these men, living close to nature; he manages to interest us in their passions, their fate, and to hold this interest through more than a thousand pages.

However, other themes were already beginning to interest Soviet writers. The Civil War was a thing of the past; now the future had to be prepared and the Socialist State constructed. What was the writer's place to be in the communal work?

At the beginning, the Soviet government was too occupied with more urgent tasks to bother much about literature, and left it fairly free. The group "The Brothers Serapion" (Zamyatin, Vsevolod Ivanov, Zoshchenko, Fedin, Kaverin) were able to write in their manifesto: "A work of art must live its own individual life; it must be authorized, but not obliged, to reflect its epoch." The Futurist group called "The Seven," of whom Mayakovsky was one, for some time commissioned by Lunacharsky to edit *The Art of the Commune,* professed to represent Revolutionary art, but it was very far removed from the mass of the people. From 1918 on, people were thinking of the creation of a proletarian literature. Bogdanov founded the Proletkult, an organization of Marxist inspiration but independent of the Communist Party; by means of reviews, clubs and courses of study, it attempted to educate the masses and to train the talents coming from the people. Gorky, who played a considerable role as a patron of literature, lent his assistance.

However, some of the proletarian writers soon found that the Proletkult put them at some distance from life and revolutionary action. The "Forge" group put form and art firmly in the background, considered literature as a weapon, repudiated individualism and exalted the industry that was to liberate the universe. They were indignant at the appearance of NEP, which favored the fellow travelers, i.e. writers who consented to go along with the Communists without sharing all their ideas (among them Vsevolod Ivanov, Pilnyak, Leonov, Fedin and Tikhonov); their revue was called *Red Soil*. These independents, who were the best writers of the time, were violently attacked by the partisans of a doggedly proletarian and Communist culture, in particular by the "October" group, which published the review *To the Post*. In May, 1924, this group brought about a special meeting of the Central Committee of the Communist Party, followed a few months later by the publication of the famous *Party Resolution in the Field of Belles-Lettres*, which was remarkably broad in its views. The Party officially repudiated "the monopoly of a single organization," declared itself in favor of "free emulation of the different literary currents," and recommended a respect for the cultural heritage of the past and for artistic technique. The fellow travelers had won their case, and the following years were to see some remarkable works from them. However, this was not the end of hostility against them. "October" had given place to "Vapp" (a pan-unionist association of proletarian writers) which contained a special Russian section called "Rapp"; at the time of the first Five-Year Plan in 1929 this redoubled its opposition. The fellow travelers were ordered to put themselves at the service of the Plan, and almost all accepted the "social commands" of the State. Their obvious sincerity and the success of the first Plan brought about, in 1932, a new relaxing of the discipline; in order to end hostility between the groups, Vapp was dissolved and all writers were thenceforth united in one association, the Union of Soviet Writers; the qualifications for entry, broadly speaking, merely demanded an undertaking to work for socialist construction by using the so-called "social realism" method. This fairly liberal formula allowed, in the years preceding the war, for very varied tendencies to appear, and a new humanism became apparent. But the exigencies of the war tightened discipline once more. It should be added that the State as sole publisher and bookseller generously rewarded a successful author, and he occupied a privileged position.

Novels on the Five-Year Plan

During the era of the first Five-Year Plan, literature devoted itself to the economic transformation of the country. F. Gladkov's *Cement,* the novel that had the largest circulation in Soviet literature, had already depicted work being started again in a factory after the Revolution. From 1929 on, a host of works of this kind appeared in praise of the creation of new industries or the collectivization of the land. Sholokhov's *Virgin Soil Upturned* and Panferov's *Brussky* glorified the kolkhoz; Katayev's *Time, Forward!* describes the huge collective organization at Magnitogorsk, Pilnyak's *The Volga Falls to the Caspian Sea* the construction of a dam, and Leonid Leonov's *Sot* the construction of a paper factory. These works have mainly a documentary interest; the best manage to rise above the too frequent stereotypes of the virtuous Communist and the vile saboteur and strikingly oppose the new world to the old, singing of labor in pages that are almost lyrical.

Satirical and Psychological Novels

Nevertheless, particularly between 1925 and 1929, other tendencies came into play and more subjective works appeared. Neither revolutionary ardor nor the enthusiasm for work could stifle the Russians' sense of humor or penchant for psychology; they were the heirs of Gogol and Dostoievsky. Self-criticism has always been encouraged in the U.S.S.R., but it is something only to be undertaken with prudence. Although Zamyatin placed the action of *We* in the sixteenth century, the work could not appear in Russia; Zoshchenko was for some time excluded from the Union of Writers, as for several years his stories had highly amused the public by making fun of certain aspects of daily life in the Soviet Union. Although often very innocently amusing, they sometimes hide more serious criticisms; the author deliberately puts them in the mouth of a Mr. X, and his language is very witty. Also very amusing are Ilf and Petrov (*The Twelve Chairs*), Katayev (*The Embezzlers*) and Bulgakov (*Devilry, The Adventures of Tchitchikov*).

The irony of Ilya Ehrenburg is above all directed against capitalist society. Having almost always lived in the West, he satisfies the Soviet public's love of the exotic by depicting and criticizing foreign countries. He is an author with a very varied and fertile imagination, and in particular a great talent for journalism. *The Fantastic Adventures of Julio Jurenito and His Followers* takes us across the whole world in the wake of a Mexican political agitator. *Trust D. E.* is a fantasy about the destruction of Europe by American mechanization; *Moscow Does Not Believe in Tears* is about the Parisian scene, and France is also the subject of Ehrenburg's novel *The Fall of Paris*, which combines severe criticism of our political environment with a genuine sympathy for our misfortunes.

Alongside this satirical energy was the desire to return to psychological analysis, to the tradition interrupted by the Revolution. This was particularly the case with the independent writers who were less absorbed with questions of politics. As far back as 1924, Fedin, in *Cities and Years*, was studying not only the struggles and achievements of the Revolution, but its repercussions in people's minds; his hero is a student who would like to become part of the new world but is dominated by his personal feelings, love and pity, and finally betrays the cause. *The Brothers* and *The Rape of Europe,* by the same author, also give a large place to individualism. Leonid Leonov's *The Badgers* (1925) personifies the conflict of town and country in the minds of two antagonistic brothers; like Fedin, Leonov is clearly more attracted by life, with "its bitter and tough tang . . . its lack of consistency and even its wise absurdity" than by doctrines.

Independence is carried even further in the work of Kaverin and Olecha. In *On an Unknown Painter* Kaverin defends the liberty to create, romanticism against utilitarianism, and moral problems against technique; defeated by life, his hero manages to survive through art. Yuri Olecha's very fine novel *Envy* (1927) contains in its fresh and entirely original few pages an extraordinary power of suggestion.

As a contrast to the loyal and active new man, he presents a failure, envious and cowardly, and nevertheless makes us feel that there is not merely baseness in this misfit, but also a need for beauty, feeling and escape. Olecha also wrote a delightful fantasy for children, *The Three Fat Men.*

Historical Novels and Novels of Fantasy

Some writers managed to escape the excessively severe realist discipline by writing novels of fantasy or historical novels. First place among them must go to Alexey Tolstoy (1882–1946), who began by emigrating with the rest, but who returned to the U.S.S.R. as early as 1922. His brilliant talents led him to attempt a wide variety of work, having in common perhaps only one characteristic: their profound devotion to everything Russian, a fervent patriotism. *The Road of Torment,* begun in Paris and completed only a few months before the author's death, is a great fresco of the Russian intellectual world before, during and after the Revolution. *Bread* describes Stalin's defense of Tsaritsyn during the Civil War. But Tolstoy's popularity was due both to his novels of Wellsian fantasy—*Aelita,* in which we see a Soviet expedition going to the aid of the Revolution on Mars, *The Revolt of the Machines, The Hyperboloid of Engineer Garin*—and even more, to his great historical novel *Peter the First.* This is a powerful work, seething with life and color; it describes the whole of Russian society at the beginning of the eighteenth century, complete with boyars, soldiers and mujiks, fanatical Old Believers and Germans of the Sloboda, and towering over all, the superhuman, revolutionary personality of the great tsar, the forerunner of the contemporary social reformers.

Historical novels multiplied in the years just before the war, encouraged by awakened patriotism and national pride, and increasing these in turn. There were novels about the rebels Stenka Razin and Pugachev, but also about Ivan the Terrible, Dmitri Donskoy and Alexander Nevsky. There were novels about recent history: Sergeyev-Tsensky described *The Suffering at Sebastopol,* Novikov-Priboy the fighting at *Tsushima.* Sentimentalized biographies were also very fashionable. Tynyavov wrote biographies of Pushkin, Kuchelbecker and Griboyedov. All this was representative of a strong movement that encouraged Russians to honor the glories of their past, on the very eve of the war that was to put their patriotism to its greatest test.

The Theatre

Since 1917 the theatre had followed exactly the same process as the novel. Always unsurpassed as far as originality of presentation was concerned, it had nevertheless, before 1917, produced few works of the first merit: Russia remained the country of the novel par excellence. Many plays were extracts from novels and made great hits. The Civil War was almost the only theme in the early stages. Gorky's last plays, *Igor Bulytchev and Co., Dostigayev and Co.,* are caricatures of the provincial bourgeoisie just at the beginning of the Revolution: the first gains its power from the vigorous personality of Bulytchev, his attitude to the imminent collapse of his world and to his own death, also approaching; the second play is stiff. Savlin's *Intervention* paints a humorous picture of the reactionary society of Odessa following the landing of the Allies. Korneychuk's *The End of the Fleet* depicts the heroism of the Black Sea sailors. Later on, propaganda plays such as Kirshon's *Bread* advocated work. Even ballets had political significance. Then gradually more and more popularity was gained by psychological plays, of which the most noteworthy are *The List of Benefits* and *A Serious Young Man,* by Olecha, and also comedies such as Katayev's *The Square of the Circle,* an amusing picture of sentimental life among students complicated by the crisis of accommodation, and finally by historical plays, such as *Ivan the Terrible,* in which Alexis Tolstoy emphasized the spirit of democracy as opposed to the pride of the boyars, and plays on Suvorov and Kutuzov.

Literature of the War

The arrival of the war gathered together and united all talent just as it had all the strength of the nation. The poets sounded the call to arms: A. Surkov, Demian Biedny, Golodny, N. Tikhonov and many others, although it must be said that their art did not often match their intentions. Issakovsky was able to capture the tone of popular poetry, and Tvardovsky in *Vassily Tierkin* the type of soldier full of *joie de vivre* even in the face of death. Simonov at times reaches a virile grandeur: all Russia knows *Wait for Me* by heart. *Days and Nights* brings to life the defense of Stalingrad (in which he participated himself) very simply and humanely; several years later he returned to his memories of the war with somber and lucid realism in *The Living and the Dead*. His plays, *People of Russia* and *A Lad from Our Town,* inspired the youth of Russia with courage. The war, in fact, gave rise to numerous dramatic works that had an even more direct effect than the novels. Korneychuk's *The Front* confronts an old soldier of the Revolution with the commandant who demands modern combat technique. Leonov's *Invasion* describes the suffering of a small occupied town, and its regeneration through the sacrifice of a young man who has gone astray, who offers his life to save the leader of the partisans; it has scenes that are movingly and dramatically intense.

Novels and narratives were even more abundant. New names were added to those of Alexis Tolstoy, Ilya Ehrenburg (the latter was extremely prolific), Sholokhov, Leonov, Katayev and Fadeyev, who were already well known. Besides national fervor, all these works have in common a determination to be clear, a simplicity, a scorn for any artifices of style: they were written for the people. In *The Volokolamsk Causeway* Alexander Bek gives a spirited and even humorous account of how an officer from Kazakstan shapes the collective mind of his battalion and turns it into a weapon of war. In *The Taking of Velikochumsk* Leonov describes without any emphasis the heroic action of a tank crew. Tikhonov describes the tranquil heroism of the population of besieged Leningrad, Katayev that of the partisans in the *Catacombs* of Odessa, and Gorbatov the indomitable hope of the people of the ravaged countrysides in *The Unsubdued*. Fadeyev's *The Young Guard* is the scarcely romanticized story of the organization and tragic end of a network of resistance formed by very young people in the

Donetz region. Ajayev's *Far from Moscow* shows another aspect of the struggle: the courage of the engineers who constructed a pipeline in Eastern Siberia amid unbelievable difficulties.

After the War

Faced with the huge task of reconstruction, the State once more appealed to literature to help stimulate work in the factories and the fields. Babayevsky's *Knight of the Gold Star,* and Galina Nicolayeva's *Harvest,* show yesterday's soldiers returning to their kolkhozes, which in the absence of any young blood have slipped into careless ways and mere routine, and inspiring them with their own energy and enthusiasm. Other novels have a mainly documentary interest, and introduce us to the new methods of the Donbas factories or of the Don River fisheries, or again, lead us among the people, who only yesterday were living in a wild state, often as nomads of Central Asia, but who today are entering the stream of modern life—without having had to pass through any transition period. All these works present youth with the ideal of working, forgetful of self, for the future of the country; they are simple, sound and have little time for sentimental complications and still less for philosophical problems. Nevertheless a tendency toward more intricate psychological study is evident not only in two fine novels of a writer of the earlier generation, Fedin's *First Joys* and *An Amazing Summer,* but also in the work of younger writers. Paustovsky, in *The Book of Life,* carries on, like Fedin, the tradition of Tolstoy and Gorky; his memories of childhood are set against charming descriptions of the Ukraine. The title of a novel by Dudintsev, *Not by Bread Alone,* is in itself a program.

A place apart must be made for *Doctor Zhivago,* by the poet Pasternak, since it was only known as a result of the translations made in 1958, and then by editions that appeared abroad. It won the Nobel Prize for its author, who had to refuse it and died shortly afterward in miserable loneliness. It in no way attacked the Revolution, which he had greeted with hope, but courageously held out for the rights of the individual and the artist. In this novel of realism and dream there are both cruel scenes and landscapes of a magical charm, a deep insight into art and human destiny, the history of an epoch and a beautiful love story; like all Pasternak's work, it is a fervent hymn to life.

If greater liberty of choice is given to Soviet literature, it can be hoped that it will spontaneously recover the great traditions of the nineteenth century, that once more it will turn its attention to the individual, without at the same time turning away from collectivism, and without renouncing the contact made with the masses of the people: a contact long sought after and at last established. Soviet literature should be enriched by this contact, and by the contributions of the many different nationalities that make up the Soviet Union.

Index

Pasternak, Boris, 126–27; *Doctor Zhivago*, 127, 140; *My Sister Life*, 126; *Safe-Conduct*, 127
Paustovsky, Konstantin: *The Book of Life*, 139
Pechersky, *see* Melnikov, Pavel I.
Peshkov, Alexis, *see* Gorky, Maxim
Peter I, Tsar, "The Great," 23–25
Petrashevsky group, 80
Petrov, Evgeny: *The Twelve Chairs*, 133
Philosophy, beginning 19th century, 55–56; religious, 61–62; Slavophiles, 59–61; Westerners, 56–59
Pilnyak, Boris, 128–29, 131; *The Naked Year*, 128; *The Volga Falls to the Caspian Sea*, 132
Pisarev, D. I., 58
Pisemsky, Alexey F.: *A Bitter Fate*, 107; *Thousand Souls*, 78; *Troubled Seas*, 78
Plays, historical, 103–4; *see also* Theatre
Plekhanov, Georgi V., 61
Poe, Edgar A., 118
Poetry, beginning 19th century, 37; epic, 5–8; introduction of verse, 26; lyric, 10–11; opposing schools after 1840, 113; "pure," 115–18; after Revolution, 123–27; as a weapon, 114–15; *see also* Acmeists, Futurists, Symbolism
Poland, and Russian cultural revival, 21
Polar Star, 38
Polejaiev, Alexander I., 50
Polevoi, 38
Polonsky, Yakov P., 117
Populist movement, 60–61
Posochkov, Ivan, 24–25; *On Indigence and Wealth*, 24
Potekhin: *The Judgment of Men Is Not the Judgment of God*, 107

Primitive Chronicle, 14–15
Printing, 22
Prokopovich, Theophan, Metropolitan of Novgorod, 24; *Saint Vladimir*, 24
Proletkult, 130
Proverbs, 9
Provincial Council (1551), 18
Pugachev, Emelyan I., 47, 136
Puppet theatre, 11
Pushkin, Alexander Sergevich, 38, 43–47; in exile, 44–45; lyric poetry, 48; Mukhaylovskoye period, 45–46; *Boris Godunov*, 45, 104; *The Brigand Brothers*, 44; *The Bronze Knight*, 47; *The Captain's Daughter*, 47; *The Captive of the Caucasus*, 44; *The Coffin-Maker*, 47; *Count Mulin*, 47; *Eugene Onegin*, 45–46; *The Fountain of Bakhchisaray*, 44; *Gypsies*, 44; *History of the Revolt of Pugachev*, 47; *The Knife*, 44; *The Little House of Kolomna*, 47; *The Negro of Peter the Great*, 47; *Novels of Belkin*, 47; *Ode to Liberty*, 44; *Poltava*, 47; *The Postmaster*, 47; *Ruslan and Ludmila*, 44; *The Shot*, 47; *To the Sea*, 44; *The Village*, 44
Pushkin, Vassily, 36, 39

Racine, Jean, 28
Radischev, Alexander N., 31–32; *Voyage from Petersburg to Moscow*, 31
"Rapp," 131
Raskolniki, 20
Razin, Stenka, 136
Red Soil, 131
Religious literature, 14, 18
Remizov, Alexis: *The Fifth Pestilence*, 101; *The Sisters of the Cross*, 101
Renaissance, in Russia, 25